FROM 'SHY BOY' TO 'SHOW OFF'

A few selected memories

WILLIAM FREEMAN

Author, Cartoonist, MC and Toastmaster

For my family.

With love and thanks to all my past and present family members and love to all those yet to come.

PROLOGUE

Tony Benn, the Labour politician was a great diary keeper. When asked why he did this, he observed that keeping a diary means that you experience life three times. Once during the experience; again, when you write about it and a third time when you later read it.

That partly explains why I wrote this book. It isn't a diary; it isn't a eulogy and it certainly isn't a novel. Rather, it is a selection of memories.

My dad was a habitual writer. When I read his diaries and letters, I wish I'd had taken the chance to talk to him about his life experiences. He was a quiet man who kept his thoughts and, particularly, his sufferings, to himself. He would never want to be 'a burden'.

He never was and never would be. I'm glad that he made dairy notes and kept the typed 'blue copies' of the letters and articles he had written. Reading about the tough lives that both he and my mother had makes me realise how lucky I have been.

I want my children and grandchildren to understand aspects of my life history and experiences and to know the kind of man that their dad / grandfather was. I'm not portraying myself as an ideal role model – far from it – I'm just giving some background information that could explain my behaviours and the things that influenced me.

Another factor, and it's an example of my 'show off and trying to impress' characteristics, I fancy being a writer and selling books and articles. These notes could produce some good material.

Maybe, deep down, I'm trying to understand myself and make sense of my personality and desire to do something 'worthwhile'.

About two thirds of these notes are about my pre-married, pre-children life. That's not to diminish the importance of my family; they are at the heart of everything I live for. Memories of the last thirty-five years or so are captured on family photos and video clips so I felt less need to repeat them as descriptive text. Few of the memories in this 'book' are captured anywhere else – although modified versions of some of them have been in published articles.

I'm probably guilty of inaccuracy, forgetfulness, selective memory and the occasional recollection through 'rose coloured' glasses. I promise to try to stay honest and not to 'big myself up' too much.

So here goes …

CONTENTS

CHAPTER 1

EARLY ARRIVAL

I have an obsession about being on time. I've been known to turn up an hour before an appointment and be happy to wait; if there's any hint that I could be late, I get anxious. I plan extra time into every travel journey 'just in case'. It's always been like that with me; and I imagine it always will be; it's part of my genetic code. At my very first appointment, true to the form that would drive me throughout my life, I arrived early; I was born on December 11th 1943, seven weeks ahead of my due date and weighing a measly 2lb 6oz. That's just over a kilo in today's money or, as my dad described it, 'not much more than a bag of sugar'. That's light even by today's standards and the hospital people called me 'their miracle baby'.

The 1946 UK Maternity Survey revealed that every single baby born less than 2lbs 3oz didn't survive - which was still the case in 1948 when the National Health Service was launched. Thankfully, I just squeezed under the bar – or was it over the bar? Whichever it was, I fell on the right side of the statistical boundary – by a mere three ounces.

Ten years later, I found out that the doctor who delivered me was amazed I had survived. I like to think that I was born for a greater purpose but time is running out for me to discover it. Maybe my 'greater purpose' is to ensure the development and security of my family.

I'll settle for that and do my best to fulfil it.

I could paint a dramatic picture of wartime bombs causing my early ejection but it wouldn't be true; my parents lived in Northumberland where bombs were rare. At first, I assumed the story of my premature birth was fabricated to justify the fact that my parents had only been married eight months when I was born. My father would smile when I joked about this in my teenage years but my mother was less amused, telling me 'that sort of thing' didn't go on in her day.

For the first six months of my life, home was a hospital incubator. For a premature baby, this special box was the next best thing to being inside its mother's belly; incubators protected us 'miracle babies' from germs that could cause sickness and infection. In 1943 they were still comparatively simple devices and, unlike hospital incubators of today, my version (my dad later told me) looked like a primitive space capsule. No wonder my mother became a successful chicken breeder in later years; I was her incubator prototype. No wonder too, that my childhood hero was Dan Dare of Eagle comic fame, who travelled the galaxy in his space ship 'incubator'.

In my early weeks, I looked like one of Dan Dare's space adversaries – blueish skin, a pointed head and without any fingernails or toenails. Quite a shock for Dad, then a young first-time father, who needed constant reassurance that I would, in time, gain weight, look normal and develop all necessary attributes. I hadn't developed the 'sucking' process that babies need when they are first born, so I was 'push' fed through, what my dad described as, a 'fountain pen filler'; force feeding at its kindest. The natural survival process for all other earthborn species wouldn't waste any time with a premature runt like me and much as I love animals, I'm very glad I'm not one of them.

My first cot was a drawer from a small wooden chest which later became part of my bedroom furniture. I was a quiet baby; my lungs couldn't generate much noise which my father told me in later years, meant that he resisted the temptation to push the drawer shut – a typical example of his humour. The old chest lasted a few years and ended its contribution to my wellbeing as part of our winter fireside fuel.

In my parents' era, choosing a child's name tended to follow tradition rather than just be a parental choice. My father was called 'Robert Henry' as was his father before him but my parents wanted to avoid any danger of me becoming 'Robert Henry Junior', or 'Robert Henry 3'. My father had revoked any such attachment to his name; which he regarded as a vulgar American custom – although he accepted that it was necessary for the Kings and Queens of England. 'Robert Ian' (their first choice of names for me) had already been allocated to my half cousin and my mother refused to 'steal' the name even though my premature birth put me ahead of him in the queue.

"What's in a name? That which we call a rose by any other name would smell as sweet," so wrote William Shakespeare, reminding us that true character stems from the person and not from the identifying label, but even he might agree that rational thought should go into the choice. A name should present the right image and not something inappropriate. For obvious reasons, 'Adolf' wasn't, and possibly still isn't, a popular name. Naming fashions have changed over time; nowadays there are exotic names like 'Primrose', 'Kyle' and 'Brooklyn'. Rumour has it that Brooklyn Beckham was so named after the place of his conception. This sort of fanciful nonsense (as Dad would have called it) didn't exist in the 1940s. Besides, being called 'Hadston Farm' wouldn't have suited me.

I was christened William David and told that I was named after my Uncle Bill. This pleased him, not because there is anything special about these names, but that he was the influence for their selection. Occasionally he would say, 'don't forget that you are named after me!' He was a fine and honest man and I liked him a lot.

So, the 'naming after someone' tradition worked well for me. Cheers Uncle Bill.

My family often joke about, what they call, my multiple or perhaps, confused identities. As a child I was called 'Billy' which evolved into 'Bill' as I grew older. The popular cartoon character 'Oor Wullie' from 'The Sunday Post' newspaper was a family favourite and my dad started calling me 'Wullie'. Lose the Scottish accent in saying and it sounds like 'Wally', the name my University friends called me. Notwithstanding, as Shakespeare implied, deep down I'm the same person whatever name I answer to.

One of our farm animals was referred to as 'Billy's cow'. I drank milk straight from this cow (not literally) but it was warm, creamy and unpasteurised (still had its natural bacteria). My parents believed that the fresh milk was good nourishment that would help me grow and that the bacteria would ward off infection. I suspect these theories were based more on my father's thinking rather than coming from sound medical advice. Anyway, it did me no harm and I did grow.

I was also fed a daily spoonful of 'Radio Malt', a government sponsored means of helping post war children to develop bulk. The big jar of treacle and molasses-like mixture was crammed with the vitamins that young children needed. The malt was a by-product of the brewing industry, derived from barley grains. It was packed full of nutrients and was a cheap dietary supplement for a generation of undernourished children who needed a high carbohydrate feed as well as more vitamins. Small wonder that in The House at Pooh Corner, Kanga gave Roo and Tigger malt extract as a "strengthening medicine".

Potter's Herbals, the UK supplier of malt extract, has now relaunched the product to coincide with the company's 200th birthday, offering malt extract with cod liver oil in three flavours: butterscotch, honey and natural, as well as malt extract alone.

I loved the wonderful toffy flavour of Radio Malt and I would force our Bakelite spoon deep into the jar to gather up as much as I could. I was also fed concentrated orange juice to pump me with vitamin C, once again courtesy of HM Government. This came in a medicine style bottle (thin and with a narrow neck). It could have been diluted with water to make a drink but my mother preferred the spoon method as it was a nice reward after my daily castor oil spoonful; another government sponsored treat!

My mother worked on the farm milking cows and churning the creamy milk into butter. Most of this was for government wartime distribution in line with the rationing rules of the day, although we managed to get a fair share for ourselves. I recall the sloshing of the butter churn as it separated the cream from the milk. It seemed quite a big device (but, then again, I was small) rather like a modern-day cement mixer. I remember too, the slap of 'paddles' as my mother patted and shaped the agitated cream into rectangles of bright yellow butter. When she wasn't doing that, she was stirring and washing clothes in a stone sink and then forcing them through a hand wound wringer ('mangle').That became my job when I was deemed strong enough but it was much later before I was allowed near the butter paddles; probably more due to hygiene concerns than a comment on my strength.

I was an only child (it was ten years before my parents dared to venture down this path again). I suspect that the intensive care in my early days made me rather spoilt and gave me an unhealthy love of being the centre of attention. "Nobody cares about Billy", I would say when the topic of conversation drifted elsewhere but I like to think that I've grown out of this trend.

Dad believed that letting nature play a strong part in my life would contribute to my health and growth. Even though food was scarce, quite a bit of what we ate was home grown. Rationing forced most people in UK to use powdered egg and powdered milk but we were able to avoid much of that. Letting me play in dirt would, in my dad's view, build my resistance to germs and infection. A grazed knee or any other such injury wouldn't be covered with a bandage or sticking plaster. It would be washed and cleaned but left uncovered. 'Let the air get at it,' was his mantra. He believed that eating the right food and having a natural involvement with nature would make me strong and healthy.

I can't fault his logic. Seventy odd years later I'm six feet two inches tall and my two pounds six ounces has grown to over 16 stones. I think that I would be a very good advertisement for 'Radio Malt'.

I await their call.

11

CHAPTER 2

DAD, CAPTAIN MARVEL AND FREDDIE FREEMAN

I've been fortunate in my life; firstly, by surviving the premature birth statistical dangers (albeit only by only three ounces) and secondly, by living through luckier times than my father. I was born on the cusp of the baby boomer era and grew up with all the privileges of government post war subsidies in housing, health and education – and during a time of optimism about the future.

The Butler 1944 Education act gave me a cost-free route through primary school education, which took me to eleven years old, and then after passing my 'eleven plus' exam, entrance to Berwick Grammar School through secondary education and onwards to University. The co-educational aspect of the school should have made me more confident with girls but my intense shyness was still a stumbling block. However, I learned to dance and perform drama events so, in these activities, I was able to make some physical contact.

I went to Bristol University with government funding for my tuition and enough money left over for accommodation and generous pocket money – and I emerged with a degree of sorts and a 'proper job'. My regular salary and employment benefits were things my father could only dream of and were never part of his working life. Like many young people of that era, I didn't understand how lucky I was nor did I appreciate the sacrifices that my parents had made. I, and my contemporaries, could live lives that the wartime generation had fought, and in many cases had died, to give us. Perhaps it is natural to take things for granted when you are young, but I really do wish that I had shown more gratitude.

Dad left school when he was fourteen years old (normal school leaving age at that time) and started work at the local coal mine. Further educational advancement wasn't an option for him and besides, the family needed his wage contribution. He started work as a 'trolley weighman' at South Broomhill Colliery (which became part of the National Coal Board after 1947 nationalisation). This was very arduous shift-based work with all the inherent physical demands and dangers of coal mining in the nineteen forties.

Dad would lie on a trolley and hurtle down a narrow tunnel to collect coal at the pit face, He would then load coal to be pulled back to the mineshaft and weighed. He joked about how lying flat on the coal trolley was similar to flying through the air like 'Captain Marvel', one of DC comic's first 'superheroes' and we would mime this as I lay across his knees. His mining friends called him 'Freddie' after 'Freddie Freeman', Captain Marvel's worldly alter-ego. In the comic world, Clark Kent went into a phone booth to change into Superman. Freddie Freeman would transform into Captain Marvel at the shout of 'Shazam'. The name 'Freeman' might have prompted my dad's nickname but perhaps his regular coal face arrival shout of 'Shazam' might have influenced it.

His miner's helmet protected his head but his back would bounce against the tunnel roof as the trolley was pulled along and coal dust would seep through his sweat-sodden vest giving him blue nodules along the top of his spine. Of course, Dad and I both knew that these weren't really coal dust marks; they were battle scars from his fights against blue-skinned aliens during his world-saving Captain Marvel excursions.

Likewise, the missing top joint of his left hand third finger wasn't the result of a mining accident, it was yet another badge of glory from his space fighting battles to save the planet. This finger doubled up as his spontaneous 'tummy tickling tool' so I had to watch it warily.

Dad was a great story-teller but he didn't have a fun tale to account for coughing up blood and for his rasping breathing.

Coal mining was probably the worst kind of work for a frail man with only one effective lung. He made light of his breathing difficulties and his coughing spasms, but my mother told me the doctor was going to send him away to get himself better. He had contracted tuberculosis partly due to living with a defective lung but mainly, I now believe, due to working in deep coal mines where lung and breathing diseases were prevalent.

His second home became 'Wooley Sanatorium', a TB treatment centre in Northumberland which started life in 1916 to treat First World War gas victims. The building was a series of barrack room dormitories, rather like a prisoner of war camp. Before he went to Wooley, my dad was given a booklet explaining the 'sanatorium procedures and rules'; a lot of time would be spent propped up in bed, Exercise was prescribed and very limited to prevent 'over-tiredness' and toilet visits were regulated. "I didn't realise I was going to a prisoner of war camp," he would tell me and he would joke about escaping if it became too bad. "Some of my mining chums will come and tunnel me out if I ask them", but I knew he didn't really mean it.

TB was fairly common in the early years of twentieth century and, as it was contagious, there were concerns about it becoming an epidemic. All sufferers were registered and closely monitored. When patient symptom reached a critical level, doctor home visits were deemed unsafe so sanatoria were set up to limit the disease and to stop it spreading. Even so, less than five per cent of sufferers were sent to sanatoria. Wooley 'inmates' (as Dad referred to himself and the other patients) were selected on some kind of priority system so that the limited space, staff and number of beds were able to cope - it's good to see that we have maintained some medical traditions over the ensuing years.

The main curative process for TB involved getting lots of rest and fresh air. Patient beds would be moved to outside verandas and, in some cases, the dormitory windows would be kept open in all weather. In truth, it would have been easy to escape without having to dig a tunnel!

Any necessary medical intervention involved 'collapse therapy' where a hole was cut in the patient's chest and air injected to collapse the infected lung. This, the theory believed, would allow the lung to rest and to recover. It was crude and painful medical treatment the memory of which traumatised Dad and at home during his recuperation; he would get panic attacks at the thought of having to undergo it again (which he had to quite often). 'Pulmonary tuberculosis was reputed to have a 50% mortality, with tuberculous meningitis and pulmonary tuberculosis uniformly fatal'. Dad wrote this sentence in his diary and, even though I don't fully understand the words or their context, I can understand his fears. Like me at my time of birth, he had to fight and win his battles against medical statistics but we would expect nothing less from 'Freddie' Freeman. Despite the trauma of his medical treatment, my father was full of praise for the medical team and for everyone who worked at Wooley.

Part of the ongoing medical recovery involved 'expectoration', where patients were required to 'spit into your mug wherever you are'. In hospital, this sputum would be analysed and used to diagnose the need further treatment or X ray requirements. Back at home, Dad carried on 'spitting for England' (looking for blood and smears) and he joked about how 'his Captain Marvel bloody spit would help win the war' but I never quite understood how.

In 1922, at the peak of a TB epidemic, the ministry of health specified that patients should make donations, or be charged, to help pay for the costs of treatment. Northumberland County Council, like many others, waived this for ex-servicemen and a hardship fund was established to pay for other specific cases and for heroes like 'Freddie Freeman'.

Walking was an important part of Dad's recuperation, partly to get exercise and partly to breath lots of 'fresh air'. The physical activity was prescribed to be gentle and to build gradually and there were guidelines on how far he should walk. It was also an important way for him to build self-confidence and to help him reduce his anxiety problems.

Most of us eventually become parents to our parents but that role reversal came to me early. I would hold Dad's hand and take him for a walk down our local country lane. The gentle pace was just right for a sick man and a young child. We would continue walking until he wanted to stop and return home. Our aim was to pass the point we had reached the previous day and after we had done that, Dad would start looking back, slowing down and eventually stopping. 'That'll do for now, Billy.' He would reach into his pocket for some chalk and leave a mark to show how far we had gone and every day we would pass the previous day's chalk mark. He also taught me a few Boy Scout woodcraft signs, involving crossed twigs and stones to show 'base camp' and to inform any passing trained tracker that we had returned home. More mundanely, it recorded our progress in case rain came and washed away our chalk mark.

Our respective roles gradually reverted to how they would normally be and he would start taking me for a walk; holding my hand and pointing out birds, flowers, plants, trees and other beauties of nature. Over the ensuing years, walking became one of his passions and we would walk for miles.

Every outing was an exploration of nature and very often included a quiz. 'What bird is that, son?' 'Do you know that plant?' His body remained frail but his mind was alert and active – especially about nature. His favourite walking stick had several supporting roles; it could beat a path when we needed one, it could chop down destructive or poisonous weeds, it could raise a barbed wire fence or it could gently expose a hidden flower or plant. This closeness to nature was very important to my dad and, in later years, I remember him telling me that he never had a strong urge to travel and how he was quite content to sit and enjoy his garden.

Today, we use the phrase 'watching grass grow' to mean something dull, boring and to be avoided. Nothing could be further from the truth in my father's eyes. "Is it better to wander the earth in search of stimulation and excitement," he wrote in his diary, "or to sit quietly in contemplation of a single flower?"

Most action heroes spend all their time being frantic and busy but 'Freddie Freeman' (aka Captain Marvel) preferred to spend his time building a good home for his family.

CHAPTER 3

MAKE DO AND MEND

◆•────────────────•────────────────•◆

During the Second World War, our supply of imported goods was under threat from enemy attack and after the war had ended, goods remained scarce while the country struggled to recover.

I was very young during the years of post war rationing (it lasted until I was ten years old) and all of this went over my head; I don't remember feeling hungry (no more than what would be expected for a growing boy) and I had clothes to wear. The aim was to keep warm; 'style' and 'fashion' weren't words that featured in anyone's vocabulary. My mother knitted pullovers, scarves and gloves often with wool unpicked from discarded items when nothing else was available. A life of home knitted pullovers, darned socks and 'hand-me-down' garments was 'normal' - not that I would have cared very much anyway. Clothes that no longer fitted my dad or my uncle Bill would be cut and modified to make garments for me.

In 1940, the Government brought in rationing to help us cope with reduced resources. Food, fuel and clothing were scarce and every adult and child in the country had a defined allocation of coupons. Government 'boffins' worked out a 'fair share for all' irrespective of status, income or wealth. This was obviously the right thing to do – even though such thoughts never entered my young head.

Dad told us that we would have to 'tighten our belts' which sounded like a way to get red lines on your tummy, but I understood his explanation so the blood supply to my lower regions was never under threat.

Clothing materials were in short supply and the priority for our manufacturing was making items needed by our armed forces. Every person in the country was given ration coupons so the Government could control the amounts of goods used. Every item in the clothes shop had a set price and a number of ration coupons allocated to it.

Clothing ration coupons came in three rather exotic colours (yellow, olive and magenta) and we were told which colours could be used at any point in time. Thinking about it now, I wonder who decided that the 'common working man' would prefer the words 'olive' and 'magenta' over the more commonly used 'green' and 'purple'. Digging a little deeper, I now know that these choices weren't decided by some high-level, artistically minded think tank, but something to do with available printing colours at the time.

Looking at my well-thumbed and now rather tatty 1947 clothing book, I see that I have eighteen unused coupons in a combination of these three (now very faded) colours. This surplus implies that I was well enough clad as far as my parents were concerned. That doesn't surprise me, as they would have surrendered some of their coupons to help me, keeping their consumption to a minimum. They would have done so not just out of parental love, but also believing that other people would benefit from their restraint. That simple act summarises my parent's lifelong generosity of spirit. I will follow their example and not regret my missed opportunities for new jacket, shirt and trousers. I'll even be proud that I forwent a new overcoat together with two sets of child sized spats ('spatterdashes') – i.e. covers to protect shoes from mud and damp.

I loved my 'tackety boots'. These were sturdy, ankle-high leather boots with metal 'tackets' on the soles. You won't find the word' tacket' in the Oxford English dictionary, Google or any other search engine. To my knowledge, it was first used by my cartoon alter-ego, 'Oor Wullie' of the Sunday Post newspaper to describe the sound his boots made on stone roads. I loved scuffing my boots on stones to make sparks fly, but this fun habit was not allowed anywhere near the hay barns.

Dad would hammer in the 'tackets' as my scuffing loosened them and I would do it myself after I had learned how to place the boot on his three-legged 'cobblers last'. No matter how you placed it on the ground, one 'leg' with a flat base would be on top, making it easy to add the boot sole face upwards. My hammering was more an imaginary game than effective shoe repair. Fun though.

My more casual footwear (apart from my slippers) was a pair of black 'sandshoes' (a Scottish word for 'plimsoll'). Two 'purple' (sorry, 'magenta') ration coupons would allow you to buy these if you could afford the price of one shilling and sixpence (about twenty-five pounds in today's currency value). These shoes had nothing to do with beaches or sand but were an early version of today's trainer, without all the modern science and designer-driven graphic artistry.

In 1944, clothes rationing meant that a man could buy a pair of socks every four months, a pair of shoes every eight months, a shirt, vest and pants every two years and an overcoat every seven years. That's pretty meagre by today's fashion purchasing habits but, even in post-war days, families had to improvise and the government's 'make do and mend' booklet became our bible.

This pamphlet was issued by the British Ministry of Information and was intended to give housewives 'useful tips on how to be both frugal and stylish in times of harsh rationing'. In truth, I think the emphasis was more on frugality than stylishness! Housewives were advised to create 'decorative patches' to cover holes in worn garments and to unpick old jumpers and re-knit alternatives. They were also encouraged to darn and alter clothing items rather than discarding them.

Mam spent her life sewing, stitching and repairing when she wasn't cooking, cleaning or working. She was the backbone of our family not just during war years but throughout her life She was 'our rock in a pinny' as I later referred to her. In those post war years, it was almost a badge of honour to have patches on your trousers - but even my mother would only go so far. A couple of patches seemed to be the limit before the garment would be cut into strips and converted to scarves, dusters, dishcloths and carpet fabric. It's ironic that a pair of fashionable jeans today, will sell with a multiple-washed worn look and 'designer tears' on the legs - in perfect condition for my mother to repair and patch up.

My parents would sit for hours threading fabric into homemade looms making colourful, blankets and rugs. I loved my patchwork scarf and ran around pretending to be 'Captain Marvel' and would have done credit to 'Joseph and his Amazing Technicolour Dreamcoat', but it hadn't yet been written.

To earn my pocket money, I would unpick damaged pullovers and then hold the wool in loops around my outstretched hands while Mam coiled it back into balls. My arms ached as I kept my elbows bent with my hands pointing upwards and I would dip my wrists alternately to force my mother to wind faster. The bribe of, 'finish this and you can listen to Dan Dare on Radio Luxembourg,' was the incentive that kept me involved.

Dad loved the phrase 'make do and mend'. It appealed to his 'fix it' nature and it became his mantra for handling any problem that had limited solutions.

"We'll just have to make do and mend", he would say and he was in his element fixing broken items, building a stool from pieces of a chair or fashioning a piece of wood to make a Boy Scout neckerchief 'woggle'. I have six of these wonderful polished and hand-painted items on my desktop today. Dad would also whittle and polish a small piece of a branch picked up from a walk to make, what he called, 'arboric art'. He would hoard every kind of item 'just in case' and was very reluctant to throw anything out. Bits of wire, old car wing mirrors, broken tools and pieces of wood were like gold dust, all to be kept until a use could be found for them. "One day, we'll be glad we kept these", he would say. We were very glad to keep them because it made him happy but years later, the out of date electrical plugs, rusty screws, broken axe handles and random pieces of lawnmower, made their final journey to the local recycling centre.

Dad's favourite jacket (his only jacket for a long while) had elbow patches that were replaced when they became worn.

Decades later, jackets with leather elbow patches became fashionable and this style of design must have been influenced by the 'wear and tear' era. My dad would have been very amused to have thought of himself as a fashion pioneer.

Over the rest of his life, Dad used the phrase, 'make do and mend' to summarise any situation where we had a problem. If the car wouldn't start, we would have to 'make do and mend' and catch the bus and if we were too late for the next bus, 'we'd have to make do and mend' and wait for the one after. We might even be forced to 'make do and mend' and use 'Shanks's Pony' – in other words, use our legs and walk.

I seem to have inherited my parents recycling instincts as I resist discarding items just because they have become worn or unfashionable or, in some cases, even broken. I'm not comfortable with today's 'throw-away and replace' culture. My mobile phone still works well and the fact that it is unglamorous compared to new items, isn't a good enough reason for me to replace it. My two laptop computers have each passed their fifth birthday and are both still functioning well - so I see no reason to replace them either.

I'm perfectly happy to follow Dad's advice and 'make do and mend'.

CHAPTER 4

'NO PUDDING UNTIL YOU CLEAN YOUR PLATE'

Whenever we get a large bill or a utility company tells us of a price increase my family wait for me to announce that 'it's now time for soup and old clothes'. Dad used this saying during the nineteen forties as we lived through post war rationing and commodities were scarce. Living on a diet of soup and wearing old clothes, even though said as a joke, was a valid way of reducing the money we spent and making the best of what we had.

Today, we enjoy the luxury of as much food as we can afford and we can buy it from any source that stocks it. Things weren't always like that. Until I was about seven years old, each person was given a set number of food ration coupons to be used in registered shops.

Typical weekly rations were

Butter: 50g (2oz)

Bacon or ham: 100g (4oz)

Margarine: 100g (4oz)

Cooking fat/lard: 100g (4oz)

Sugar: 225g (8oz)

Meat: 12ozs (350g)

Milk: 2 pints (1200ml)

Tea: 50g (2 oz)

Cheese: 2oz (50g)

Eggs: 1 fresh egg

Dried eggs: 1 packet (12 eggs) every four weeks plus various other powdered and dried items

These ration allowances were planned to give the best possible diet during the tough war years and later analysis showed that the general health of the nation was better than it had been, although the starch in the powdered elements of rationing had caused increased flatulence. I've been using this excuse for over sixty years and I apologise for my contribution to ozone layer damage. I blame Hitler.

Sweet rationing lingered on until 1954 (until I was almost eleven years old. My weekly quarter pound of Turkish delight bought from Woolworths store was, indeed, a delight and would be gobbled up during my half-hour bus ride home from Berwick on Tweed. If I paced myself, I could make my bag of a dozen cubes last the ten-mile bus journey.

We were also encouraged to 'Dig for Victory' to make every garden and patch of land an allotment so we could become as self-sufficient as possible. The Ministry of Agriculture and Fisheries initiated an educational campaign using leaflets and guides along with numerous short films, encouraging people this. The films were shown before the main feature in cinemas.

It's impossible to imagine a father, today, praising his son (as mine did) for digging up the lawn to be a vegetable patch, but the 'Dig for Victory' campaign encouraged that activity.

Susie, my wife, jokes about how I am a reluctant gardener these days. I am getting slower and older at, what seems like, an alarming rate but I attribute my reluctance to all the gardening work I did as a child in the nineteen-forties!

We, (us young boys – not girls!), would work as 'beaters' when the shooting took place. Our job was to march through the woods startling the birds so they flew up and became targets. It was quite good fun and we got lots of lemonade and sandwiches, half-a-crown (twelve and a half pence in today's money) and, if the shooters had a good day, also a pheasant to take home.

When we moved to Norham, at ten years old, I worked as a potato picker from time to time. The plough would dig up the ground and each person had a marked section of the field. A 'stint' of twenty-two yards. The job of the picker was to bend down and put the potatoes into sacks. I had half a stint and got ten shillings and sixpence (just over fifty pence for my eight hours work). And a very sore back.

Catching rabbits was another way we tried to add to our food larder. There were plenty of these, and my friend Adam, who lived on the same row of cottages had a few 'pet' rabbits that were destined to become 'pot' rabbits in due course!

Today, corn harvesting machines cut the crop in neat rows, moving in a zig-zag from the outside toward the centre. When I was a boy, the machines drove around the perimeter in ever reducing squares forcing the rabbit population to collect at the centre and the men would club them with big sticks when they ran out.

If you've have seen the early Arnold Schwarzenegger movie, 'The Running Man' you can picture what I mean. Sort of.

I was a very reluctant rabbit clubber. I would be there, of course, making all the right noises but valiantly missing with every stroke – a habit I seemed to have transferred to my golf and cricket play.

My mother's rabbit stew was a nourishing luxury that didn't involve either ration coupons or money.

Towards the end of the nineteen forties, the number of rabbits had grown to the extent that they were regarded as a 'pest' and various means were used to control numbers.

If you have read 'Watership Down', or seen the film, you will know about rabbit 'snares'; wire traps that would trap a creature and cause intense agony as it tried to free itself, tightening the noose in the process. Even when some of us kids would try to free a rabbit, it would struggle in terror and make its injuries far worse. The only solution then was to club the poor creature to death. I would fetch one of the farm workers to do this; it upset me and I couldn't watch.

The dreaded myxomatosis was a type of pox virus that only affected rabbits. It was first discovered in 1896 in Uruguay and was deliberately imported to Australia in 1951 to control its large rabbit populations - initially having the desired devastating effect. The disease was illegally introduced to France in 1952 and it appeared in Britain the following year.

Wikipedia summarises the disease as being fatal to rabbits with a 99% mortality rate. Symptoms include swollen eyelids, lips, and genitals, a high fever, lethargy, and progresses to difficulty breathing, and death, within two weeks. It was an awful sight to see and the only kind solution was to put the poor creature out of its obvious misery. More tears from me, but I was eventually able to wield the club.

Despite our comparative luxury, food was scarce and not something to be wasted. Scraps were rare. I would be told, politely but firmly, that there would be 'no pudding until you've cleaned your plate'. Today's concept of eating until you have had enough and not persisting until every morsel is consumed, is a habit I can't get into; hence I tip the scales more than I should.

I blame Hitler for that too.

CHAPTER 5

THIS LITTLE PIGGY

'This little piggy went to market, this little piggy stayed at home, this little piggy had roast beef and this little piggy had none. This little piggy went wee, wee, wee all the way home'.

This rhyme, allegedly, started in France and the 'wee, wee' wee' is really 'oui, oui, oui' (what the piggy was saying 'yes' to, I can't imagine).

The third little piggy in the lyrics that supposedly had 'roast beef' was a fantasy to many people of my generation; few of us in those days enjoyed that luxury. My mother's version, and that of many other mothers, was 'this little piggy had bread and jam', which gave a more accurate picture of our situation. My family are amused when I give this interpretation. At first, they thought I was having a joke and laughed; they found it even funnier when they realised I was telling the truth.

This ditty reminds me of wartime food rationing and the Government's 'Pig Club' initiative to encourage family pig farming.

Wartime circumstances forced us to become as self-sufficient as possible; we fished in streams and rivers, we picked mushrooms and berries. We kept chickens to give us eggs (and meat) and we formed collective and individual 'pig clubs'. Each farm cottage where we lived had an allocated pig pen.

'Pig Club' rules were quite simple. Every pig had to be registered and the authorities tracked and controlled what happened to the meat. As a family, we were allowed one pig for personal use in any given season. Others, if we had them, became part of the Government food sale and distribution process. Most families would only have one pig.

Every bit of food waste went into our 'pig swill' bucket and what we didn't use was collected by the 'pig swill' man for use on the farm. 'Pig Swill Eric' was cheery chap with, what seemed like, permanently brown stained forearms and a distinctive 'aura'. There was something strangely comforting about the sweet smell of pig swill. Just thinking of those childhood days brings that smell into my memory.

Government collections of waste and the strong encouragement of pig clubs promoted the wartime message that every scrap of resources was vital. By 1940, wasting food was deemed to be a criminal offence – an academic concept as such a thought was alien to everyone living through those years.

In the 'war on waste' people saved kitchen scraps for the communal pig bin or to feed hens for eggs. A Ministry of Food advertisement summed up the situation in this poem about pigs:

'Because of the pail, the scraps were saved,

Because of the scraps, the pigs were saved,

Because of the pigs, the rations were saved,

Because of the rations, the ships were saved,

Because of the ships, the island was saved,

Because of the island, the Empire was saved,

And all because of the housewife's pail.

Joe and Eddie were our self-appointed farm slaughters. They weren't paid to do the job but they were given a pack of home-made sausages. I remember them as nice young men but, to my sensitive eyes, they seemed to take barbaric delight in organising the killings. A circle of people would surround the pig pen exit trapping the terrified, screaming animal for Joe and Eddie to do their dastardly deed in ways that would be banned today. I think it was part of their 'macho' nature to make the pig killing a public spectacle; they would have been in the front row in the days when we hanged criminals. I'm probably being unfair and writing this with the benefit of hindsight and influenced by today's values but I wonder why the poor creature couldn't have been dispatched whilst in the sanctity of its own pen. Making it run around and squeal before they could bring it down with a mallet and then cut its throat seemed to be an unnecessary and barbaric part of the ritual. I stood with the other children and forced myself to join in the cheering and jeering but deep down, I hated the whole spectacle.

'You don't have to watch this, son' my dad would tell me but I had to really. I couldn't sit inside and hide away.

Once killed, the creature was shaved in scalding water, beheaded, disembowelled and every element of its body carved and put in the appropriate pile for subsequent cooking. Very little was wasted. All of this was done on the cobbled yard outside our little row of cottages and the blood was washed away by hose to the nearby land.

We didn't have refrigerators in those days so the pig meat was cooked quickly or packaged in salt for the cold storage room.

Our unlucky 'stay at home piggy' had been starved ('this little piggy had none') to minimise digestive effluent and waste. A 'roast beef' piggy (or even a 'bread and jam' one) would be fattened for sale and eventually became the piggy that went to market.

Joe and Eddie were also our 'Burke and Hare' style body snatchers. Extra carcasses from 'unregistered' animals would move by wheelbarrow along the back gardens to avoid the visiting inspector's tally.

My Grandfather often told the tale when he discovered two left halves of pig body in his store, just ahead of the inspector visit – too late to engage Joe, Eddie and their wheelbarrow. No amount of rearranging in the salt store could make two left halves look like they came from a single pig.

Our two barking sheepdogs, trained to follow my Grandfather's subtle signals caused enough distraction to stop the inspector looking too closely.

I don't think any little piggy shouted 'oui, oui, oui' ('yes, yes, yes') after we had fooled the inspector but, reputedly. my Grandfather did!

CHAPTER 6

PRIMARY SCHOOLDAYS

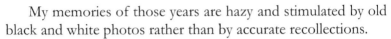

My memories of those years are hazy and stimulated by old black and white photos rather than by accurate recollections.

One memory lodged in my brain and which gets magnified every time I tell it was the time a horse kicked my head. This has become a standing joke in my family and sometimes cited as the cause of my occasionally eccentric behaviour. I picture Mam at the top of a hill, wearing a white pinafore, waving her arms and Harry Swainston, a farm worker, running towards me. In truth, I was told later that I had crawled near a pony and it flicked its front foot, brushing me slightly. Harry did rescue me though and I still have a small scar on my chin.

In 1948 we moved to South Berrington farm and Mam was employed as cook and poultry manager at 'the big house'. As part of the deal we were given a small terraced cottage; I don't know if we paid rent. We were in a small street complete with communal outside lavatory (more on that later) although, by then, each house had flushing WC. We were bang in the middle, being house number four in a street of seven.

There were other children in our little street, Adam and Margaret Black and Marjory Steel. Doors were open and we would run in and out of houses and it was normal for us to play outside. I enjoyed our outdoor play but I was also very happy in my own company (I still am). These were the days before TV (before electricity, even). We had radio (it was called 'wireless' in those days and powered by 'acid batteries'). I read books and comics, made models and could slip into flights of fancy with an old jar, a piece of string and a few marbles.

Dad was away quite a lot in my early years, partly due to illness and partly when he went on a training course at the Commercial College in Southend. Mam would go off every evening to collect eggs from the eight hen houses, leaving me at home with my Border Collie dog 'Prince'. I was comforted by his presence and felt secure, but on one occasion wandered outside to look for her. In my head, I was tracing Mam's steps and activities trying to anticipate where she would be; my imagination ran riot and I started to worry where she was. Our next-door neighbour, Mrs Wilson (I think it was) took me in until Mam returned.

The autumn after we moved to South Berrington, I went to my first school in a small village called Bowsden, about three miles away.

Two other children, Adam and Margaret Black (from number six) would walk with me to the 'road end'; this was a junction with the main road (if you can call the now named B6525 a main road) where we would be picked up by a lady in a red saloon car and taken to school - and we would do the reverse route when we were dropped off at the same place after school.

This walk was a great distance in my memory but it was probably no more than a quarter of a mile.

We were collected by a jolly lady who wore bright red lipstick. She would arrive from the North appearing over the crest of a hill from Ancroft village. The hill was called 'Bride's Brae' ('brae' being a Scottish word for hill) and was so named after a tragic accident in 1814 when a bride was being driven in a pony and trap down this steep road on their way to her wedding. Archives tell us that, something startled the pony which bolted down the 'brae' causing the trap to overturn, killing the bride. Our school car driver would often greet us with, 'well I made it up Bride's Brae', referring to the accident that gave the hill its name.

Rumour has it that the bride's ghost haunts the lonely road at night searching and calling for her husband to be. Our return from school brought us near the area and we would run home during the dusk evenings.

The notorious hill was quite gentle in my youth as the road levels were altered in 1920 to make it safer.

At the beginning of the week, I would take my dinner money. The word 'lunch' hadn't been invented – at least not in our social circles. Mam would wrap a few coins in paper and apply a generous amount of Sellotape to stop it being lost. I think the contribution was voluntary and, in some cases, kids would forget to bring it (accidentally or deliberately) but they still got fed. Some kids also brought a 'ten o'clock'; a snack provided by their mothers to 'keep them going' – probably a hangover from war years.

When my mother became a dinner lady at Norham School (our next home location several years later), she made that sure every child got a good meal with or without money.

The Education Act 1944 made it a duty of local education authorities to provide school meals and milk. This was so we post war children got some necessary nutrition and we were given a third of a pint of milk during our mid-morning break.

In later years (1968) Edward Short the labour Secretary of State for Education, withdrew free milk from secondary schools. In 1971, his successor, Conservative Margaret Thatcher withdrew free school milk from children over seven years old, earning her (among her enemies) the nickname 'Thatcher, the Milk Snatcher', probably quite unfairly as the driving force to do this was Prime Minister Ted Heath.

The authorities that deemed we should have this milk would have been horrified by our rituals. We would stand in a circle holding our milk bottle and, using the thumb knuckle from our other hand, push out the bottle top and start drinking as fast as we could to see who could finish first. I don't think I ever won but I suffered from a few indigestion problems. Lactose intolerance hadn't been invented in those days.

Even at this first school, we were taught about foraging and making the best use of natural resources. This had been a big drive during the war years and we would collect wild berries, gooseberries and apples. Rose hips were a good source of vitamin C and schoolchildren were rewarded for collecting them. A pound in weight would earn three old pence (just over a penny in today's money) and ten pounds in weight would get you the coveted rose hip collector's pin badge. These collections produced bottles of rose hip syrup with were given to families as a post-war source of vitamin C and also sold in chemist shops. Seventy years later; I don't get any cash for my foraging efforts (or even a badge) but I do get the chance to enjoy Susie's wonderful jellies and jams.

Learning by 'rote' was standard in my early schooldays. In later years I would recite 'amo', 'amas, 'amat', 'amamus', 'amatis', 'amant' as part of my Latin learning (I hope that's correct!). Miss Mather's 'clock' helped me to learn my numerical 'times tables'. She would draw a clock-face on the blackboard and put a number (e.g. nine) within the circle at the centre. This was the 'times table' we were learning. Miss Mather's cane (only used for this purpose, never for punishment) would touch an outer number (e.g. 'seven') and we would recite, "nine sevens are sixty-three". Ten minutes of that every day (maybe longer) has kept these numerics solid in my head for over seven decades. We also learned spelling by knowing the sound of each letter, so C 'cuh', A 'ah', T 'tuh', thereby spelling CAT. There was a while, during my children's infant school years when this 'phonics' method became unfashionable and was replaced by a 'whole word' approach, where children were expected to recognise complete words. Utter tosh, in my opinion and, as far as I know, it is no longer used.

One day the hounds and huntsmen came past our school and (at my instigation, I now confess) we left the playground to chase after them. In my mind we ran for miles but in reality, I suspect we ran less than a hundred yards as the teachers didn't seem to notice that we weren't there.

We played in the concrete schoolyard so grazed elbows and knees were quite common. As well as patches on our jumpers many of us boys had sticking plaster patches on our knees. I had those and more and during one game, I fell and dislocated my wrist. I can remember feeling shocked and a bit sick looking at my 'S' shaped arm. We didn't call ambulances much in those days

33

and I bounced in the back of a teacher's car during the twenty minutes journey to Berwick infirmary with misshapen arm! The anaesthetic was primitive compared to today – I was given a sort of WW2 pilot's face mask and can remember inhaling strong smelling 'gas' – and I dreamt of a suited man pulling at my fingers and woke up with a plaster cast on my arm. I loved the attention it gave me and was rather sad when it had to come off.

CHAPTER 7

NETTY, PRIVY AND NIGHT SOIL

◆●━━━━━━━━━━●━━━━━━━━━●◆

At South Berrington, our house was 'number four in a street of eight cottages. We were in the middle (sort of).

The farm cottages had been upgraded with flushing lavatories a few years earlier but a communal outside lavatory stood at the beginning of our 'Street'. We referred to it as 'the netty' (no idea why) but a more common colloquialism is 'privy'. It was the first building you saw as you turned the corner from the main road, making it seem like a very important building (and for the days prior to in-house sanitation, it probably was).

The farm houses stretched down on the right-hand side and you looked out from the 'privy'. There was a cobbled path, about ten yards wide (too narrow and unmade to be called 'street') and each house faced an individual coal shed and pig-pen. The road stopped at the end cottage (number eight) followed by rough ground and a path to a small stream.

The blacksmith's forge (the second most important building) was, literally, a 'stone's throw' from the communal privy. More accurately, a 'horseshoe throw' away as it was the landing point for the horseshoe-based quoits game that I played with my street friends, Adam, Margaret and Marjory. Adam was a few months older than me and considered himself to be the gang leader. The girls were slightly younger – and being girls, didn't show any leadership ambitions. I was, of course, the brains of the group and decided what games we played.

The privy was sited at the entrance to our street so workers of days gone by could 'do their business' before going into their houses.

There was a gap at the bottom of the rear wall for users to shovel soil over their 'contributions'. In Tudor England, this 'privy' output, together with slops from home bedpans (hence the phrase 'slopping out') was known as 'night soil' - a historically used euphemism for human excreta collected from cesspools, privies, pail closets, pit latrines, privy middens and septic tanks. This material was removed from the immediate area, usually at night, by workers specifically employed to do this unsavoury task.

Human effluent collection is still common in rural areas today for buildings without connected sewerage systems (such as our house at Heacham, North Norfolk). Lavatories flush human waste into an underground storage tank, or purpose-built soil pit, and a specialist tanker would come along from time to time and drain it out. The effluent was then used to fertilise crops after treatment to remove harmful bacteria.

In Andy Weir's award-winning book 'The Martian' the marooned hero, played by Matt Damon in the 2015 movie, survived by using his personal lavatorial waste as fertiliser to grow potatoes. The science, as explained in the book, assumed that everything, including potential diseases, would be personal to our hero and therefore not harmful, so no bacterial treatment was necessary. The author had researched this with NASA and it was deemed to be a valid solution to such a desperate situation.

Is this now part of NASA strategy to grow food as we colonise planets in the future? It won't affect me but I rather hope not! How will they practise this in the simulator?

Human waste has been a historical cause of disease (and still is in poor parts of the world) and the modern flushing water closet and sewerage processing systems rank pretty high in the table of important inventions.

As kids, we were oblivious to how the lavatory had evolved. To us, the outside privy was a play area; it was a popular 'hide and seek' location, although the places to hide were limited. If you were small enough, it would be possible to drop down the hole and escape via the opening at the bottom although, to my knowledge, no-one was ever brave enough to try it. Even so, we could never resist the urge to peek down the hole during our hide and seek adventures.

We would also stick our heads down the bowl to try to look out through the bottom opening. An impossible task but Adam and I enjoyed how it made the girls pigtail touch the soil below. My home-made periscope from a Cub Scout Annual design gave us new and exciting worlds of play. 'Lower Periscope', we would shout, rather like an upside-down submarine commander.

We used this establishment during our play rather than going back to our houses, as did the blacksmith and the occasional passing farm worker. Dad took it on himself to make sure there was a plentiful supply of neatly torn newspaper squares dangling on a loop of string. This gave him an excuse to recite his mantra of 'use only three squares; one up, one down and one polish'.

Cheap newsprint paper was softer and more bio-degradable than the shiny Izal sheets we had indoors. That was the incentive that motivated us to contribute to the supply of 'night soil'.

A valid motivation, but not as strong as that for our fictional Martian hero.

CHAPTER 8

FIRES FOR WARMTH, HOT WATER AND COOKING

A blazing fire was the heart of our home and the focal point of our 'living room' (a modern phrase to describe our only downstairs room apart from the kitchen and scullery). This fire gave us warmth; dried our clothes and boiled our kettle. There's something in the human 'psyche' that gets security and comfort from staring into the glowing embers of a natural fire. I miss it today.

It was lit most days of the year, apart from the rare warm summer days. Our living room fire in Berrington, where I lived from age four to ten, was set inside a black 'grange'. This was a forerunner to today's 'aga' and the central fire heated an oven and had a hot plate area for pans.

First thing every morning, we removed the ash and debris and prepared the fire for the new day. Mam would place strips of newspaper at the bottom, followed by crumpled pages, wood kindling and, finally, a few lumps of coal before setting it alight. Just thinking about it brings back the smell of wood smoke and how my eyes would prick as the flames took hold. My aged eyes prick again today (for sentimental reasons) as I picture Mam kneeling at the hearth and laying the fire.

I didn't mind pages of the 'Newcastle Journal' being used but I kept a watchful eye to make sure the 'Sunday Post' pages with 'Oor Wullie' and 'The Broons' cartoon stories were spared for my scrapbook. One double-spread sheet of newspaper was used to 'draw' the fire. Mam would hold it in front of the flames (carefully) and I was fascinated how the paper resisted being sucked up the chimney. I learned later that this sucking effect was caused by the rising hot air that, in turn, pulled new air to replace it, encouraging the flames to grow. Mam didn't understand any of this, bless her. She would just giggle when I asked.

Every few weeks, the coalman arrived with fresh sacks for our coal bunker. These men had grubby faces (did their mothers make them wash their faces as often as I had to?) and they wore hats with flaps at the back to protect their necks as they lifted sacks from the lorry.

This headgear reminded me of 'Luck of the Legion' from the 'Eagle Comic' and the Kepi hats they wore. This Eagle cartoon was sponsored by a date company ('Eat Me'?) and I collected the necessary number of labels from date boxes to send with a 1/6d postal order (about 15p) to get my 'Luck of the Legion' Kepi hat.

I would carry coal inside from our outside bunker – wearing proper headgear of course. I could only manage a few lumps at a time in a bucket, so the headgear wasn't a practical necessity but it helped me build my character performance. My contribution to this job was fairly small as Mam and Dad did most of it – but at least I wore the proper uniform.

My more important role was gathering small twigs and helping Dad to chop pieces of wood for kindling. His axemanship lessons stay with me today, which I'm sure I've repeated to my family on more than one occasion.

'Bounce the wood and axe together to get started, don't swing the blade'. 'Carry the axe by the blade, never by the handle'.

Every few months, a sweep would come and clean the chimneys in our little street. A brush was shoved up the chimney and I would shout when it appeared outside the top pot as the signal to pull it back down. This was quite a messy process without the benefit of modern self-contained vacuum systems. Mam would cover our floor and furniture with dust sheets and, after the seep had left, spend the rest of the day cleaning.

Once in a while, a chimney would catch fire and flames would appear from the chimney pot. Burning wood created a creosote type substance that lined the chimney and this was very flammable. Nothing dramatic happened and we all watched and waited until it burnt itself out. I heard tales of fire engines pumping water down the chimney pot but I never experienced this excitement, sadly.

Every Friday, Mam would boil water on the grange and fill up a tin tub for my weekly bath. I don't recall my parents doing this (maybe they did it during the night?) but I had to suffer this ritual (whether I needed it or not!).

Like everyone in our little street, our front door was never locked so, from time to time, my bathing was interrupted by Betty Swainston – a farm worker and jolly cow maid. I kid myself that she did this deliberately and I would rush to cover my modesty.

I doubt if this gave her much of a thrill and, besides, I suspect she had more luck with some of the adult farm workers.

CHAPTER 9

LIGHT SOUND AND VISION

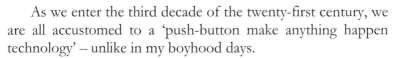

As we enter the third decade of the twenty-first century, we are all accustomed to a 'push-button make anything happen technology' – unlike in my boyhood days.

The 'wireless' gave us music and entertainment; it was so called (apparently) because there weren't any wires connecting it to the transmitting station. As electromagnetic transmission technology became more sophisticated, the humble 'wireless' took on the title of 'radio'. It was still wireless in the original context but the means of transmission had changed. As an ex-physics student, I should be able to spout detail, but I can't. So there.

Our family wireless was a large wooden box structure that took pride of place on our sideboard and it was powered by an acid accumulator battery. This was a big square glass jar about twice the size of a milk bottle, with a carrying handle. Like everyone, we had two of these. One lived inside the wireless doing its job whilst the second on was being charged. Every Saturday, these items were swopped and I would take the one from the wireless to the garage in the village and leave it to be charged, rather like a car battery is today. It cost one shilling, as I recall. We could have managed with only one of these devices but a delay in the battery charging process would cut off our radio entertainment. Imagine missing the Saturday evening radio play!

If I could remember anything of my schoolboy physics (instead of pretending I can) I would be able to explain how this acid-soaked copper (?) and lead(?) gave the current that would power the valves in the wireless.

These were like modern light bulbs and would glow and get warm as the current came through them and they would amplify the incoming signal. I would stare at these glowing valves as my imagination took flight during the afternoon play.

Dad was a big fan of 'Friday Night is Music Night' and he would 'tum-te-tum' along with the music. (not always in perfect time). My favourite programme was the Radio Luxembourg 'Dan Dare' serial which ran seven nights a week from 1951 to 1956. I imagined myself as the famous hero who with his side-kick Digby saved the human race from the evil Mekon and his army of Treens. When the Eagle Comic was launched in April 1950 with 'Dan Dare Pilot of the Future' as the lead story, I was hooked and have been ever since. I have quite a few Eagle Annuals and facsimile Dan Dare story books. I also own an original first issue of the Eagle comic (14 April 1950) framed and hanging on my wall.

The Dan Dare serial was based on the Eagle comic adventures and gave storylines with cliff-hanger endings that had me keen to hear the next episode. This 'keep-them-hanging' technique became the model for the much later TV serials.

The weekly 'Radio Times' magazine published the timetable for BBC broadcasts and was a vital magazine to help listen to a football match commentary. There was no television in those days but the BBC came up with a simple but ingenious scheme that allowed listeners to follow the action.

The Radio Times printed a reference grid that divided the pitch into numbered sectors. While the commentator described what was going on, his background partner would call 'four' or some appropriate number telling the listeners where the action was happening. This worked well and is one of the theories for the origin of the expression 'Back to Square One'.

The grid was identical for every game but the RT page had team lists and diagrams of the ground location that were unique. We bought the RT every week for the schedule of broadcasts – and for Dad to reassure himself that his beloved 'Friday Night is Music Night' would still be performed.

Before electricity, our main sources of evening light were candles and mantle lamps. These looked very nautical and a fuel lit flame heated the 'mantle' - a cone cup of wired fabric that had been soaked in chemicals making it give a bright white light when heated. These were sensitive items; they came in packets and if you touched the surface of the mantle, there was a strong chance you'd damage it.

The arrival of electricity in 1949 at our South Berrington farm cottage was preceded by a great upheaval involving a team of men lifting floorboards and digging grooves into walls and ceilings for the wires.

The day of 'turn on' started with huge excitement. We flicked on all the switches first thing in the morning and waited, looking regularly at the single central lightbulb to make sure we hadn't missed it.

It was mid-afternoon before the central bulb fizzled with a dim light. Our cheers and celebrations were as loud and vigorous as for a modern street party; we rushed in and out of all the identical cottages to stare at an identical glowing light bulb hanging from the centre of an identical ceiling.

I think we left lights on all night worried that if we switched them off, they might not come on again.

Our first electrically powered radio was a large piece of furniture as I recall and had pride of place in our sitting room – the only downstairs room we could sit in apart from the kitchen and lavatory. Ours was only a radio and not a 'proper stereogram'. That word has several different meanings today from a style of art / photography and the name of a pop group. In the context I'm writing here, a stereogram was a combination of radio and record player with storage space for LP, EP albums and individual 78 rpm double-sided vinyl records.

I would be ten or eleven years old when I got my first Dansette record player; a red and grey vinyl coated machine that would hold a stack of six or seven records and let them drop on to the turntable in sequence. This was the iconic record player of the nineteen fifties and sixties and the autochanger (the mechanism that let a record drop onto another on the turntable) was especially useful for the 'forty-five' rpm (revolutions per minute) single records. Side one was the 'A' side, the main title that was played on radio and we teenagers, as I would eventually grow into, wouldn't often know what was on the 'B' side. You could stack half a dozen singles before they started to slip on the turntable.

Before my Dansette, we had an old HMV Gramophone with a wind-up handle for our ten inch 'shellac / vinyl' singles that played at seventy-eight rpm. The revolution speed was set based on the capabilities of motors and gears at the time.

I still have a few of these old vinyls; old Scottish songs, some classical and a few Elvis Presley gems.

In late nineteen sixties, the Dansette company stopped production and more sophisticated stereo hi-fi turntable players became the norm.

The first record I bought to play was 'Tom Dooley' by the Kingston Singers.

Dad rigged wires to my player so we could connect speakers downstairs in the living room, but my record choices weren't always deemed suitable.

I (we) still have a large collection of long-playing vinyl records from Susie's and my collection and a good classical batch that came from her father's estate.

Over the last ten years, I have bought and sold a few Dansette players on eBay. A well restored model can fetch hundreds of pounds today. I wish I had kept one of them!

Television came to our village around nineteen fifty-three when I was nine years old. It was black and white and with only one channel (BBC). Every Saturday evening, I would watch the Lone Ranger at Mrs Wharton's house (a village neighbour). We would huddle round a small screen and the programme ran from 5.30pm to 6pm and then the TV would be blank for an hour.

At eleven o'clock the BBC would play the National Anthem to signify the end of broadcasting for the day. One lady in the village never turned off her set ('they turn it off for you when they're done').

A year later we got our own TV set. My father experimented with a Perspex sheet that had a strip of blue at the top, brown in the middle and green at the bottom. This was his way of getting colour TV years before it was released. Eccentric (now I know where I get that trait) but it was surprisingly realistic for outdoor scenes; less so for indoor views.

There was a while when Dad would watch TV with the image reflected in a large mirror on the opposite wall. That too, worked OK – apart from text being backwards. He had concerns about the possible radiation impact from looking directly at the TV. Eccentric? Perhaps a little – but who's to say he was wrong!

CHAPTER 10

NORMAL DANGEROUS CHILDHOOD PLAY

◆•——————————•——————————•◆

For the first ten years on my life, most normal childhood play was outside and the weather would have to be fairly severe for me to want to come indoors. These were the days before television and computers – and radio entertainment tended to be confined to the evening (apart from the weekly 'afternoon play').

Despite all that, I was a bit of an indoor child and happy to do things on my own. I still am – happy to do things on my own that is, not still an indoor child.

I enjoyed reading – Dickens, Neville Shute, Rider Haggard and Robert Louis Stevenson and many of these books still sit on my bookcase. My other indoor passions were making model airplanes, fretwork and playing with Meccano and train sets, but I was, like other kids, encouraged to get out in the fresh air while it was still light.

"Get you head out of a book and get some fresh air!" I never understood why the air inside the house wasn't deemed to be fresh, it was certainly cold enough.

My childhood world of play would fail the typical 'health and safety' checks that we have today. We waded in the stream at the bottom of our street and we climbed trees in the local woods – and fell from a few. Most falls were at the beginning of the climb as we tried to get to 'base one'; the first main 'V' that most climbable trees have. Or at the end as we hastened down from the same 'V' point.

Nettle stings were common but we knew the 'dock leaves' and spit cure. Mother Nature always seems to make sure that they grow near nettle patches. There was little danger of sunburn in the North of England, frostbite was more likely but, despite that, most boys wore short trousers until they were eleven or twelve years old. Even in later years, Dad would urge me with 'Get your day shorts on and build your hardiness!' – whatever that was. I don't recall ever seeing Dad wearing his 'hardiness building shorts'.

Sun cream wasn't applicable in the Scottish Border climate (besides, it hadn't yet been invented) but Vaseline was a Godsend for our chapped and scratched legs.

We would build 'dens' from branches and leaves which were surprisingly waterproof and warm, but our parents drew the line at letting us stay overnight in them. That pleasure came in later Boy Scout years.

Farm machinery was like a park playground to us, offering things to climb on and I enjoyed sitting on the tractor mudguards as our neighbour Joe Hills drove it (slowly, I admit).

Farm buildings were great for games of hide and seek; we would scramble up ladders and crawl under hay and loose bags; no wonder I suffered with itchy skin. We had the urge to jump into the big pit holding the grain; it looked tempting but (thankfully) something held us back. This might have been a rare display of instinctive common sense, or maybe we had been warned not to do so. We were mischievous and active kids, but obedient too.

Our ventures outside usually included a visit to the blacksmith's forge; I think it was the heat that attracted us. This building stood at the beginning of our row of cottages near the privy and just at the entry to the farm. We would pop in when the blacksmith was working and he would let us take turns to pump the bellows to the fire which he used to soften the horseshoe metal. There was something magical about the heat, the noise of hammering on the anvil and the hiss of steam as the shoes were cooled in cold water. Our starting cold faces would get red and hot from the fire and then prickly and damp from the steam.

There's a fascination watching horses being hooved. The blacksmith would hold the horse's foot up between his thighs and fasten the shoe (that he had heated, banged, shaped and cooled) to the hoof with large nails. And the horse didn't feel a thing.

There were always a few spare horseshoes lying outside the forge for local men (and us) to play quoits – or, in our case, try to.

A horseshoe is viewed as being a lucky symbol. Legend has it that the devil appeared and demanded shoes for his feet. The blacksmith took a burning hot shoe and nailed it to the devil's hoof. The pain was so intense that the devil ripped it off and swore he would never come near such an item again. Utter rubbish, of course - but the farm cottages kept one at the front door to keep evil spirits away and you often see them as good luck charms at weddings.

Our signal to come inside from our play was when Adam Black's father (the farm shepherd) blew a loud whistle at about 7pm. Then we would stop climbing trees, building dens, playing on machinery and other activities that wouldn't be allowed today – and return home.

During winter months, we were sometimes 'snowed in' which meant we couldn't get to school. Hooray! Snow could be two feet deep and we had great fun digging a path from our front door and a channel so we could walk up the road. That was the stated intention but we really wanted to make a 'slide'; an icy path that we could run at and whoosh down with the studs ('tackets') in our boots generating sparks. Nowadays, the powers-that-be would force us to wear helmets, knee and elbow pads. It would probably be illegal to build our 'slide' on a communal footpath.

We would have laughed at modern safety attitudes - even the adults would have a go on our slide.

It wasn't a dangerous game that tore my arm, it was an act of silliness. I was about ten years old and we were staying on holiday with Billy Ingledew and his family. Billy was best man at my parents' wedding but I always referred to him as my uncle. Mam, Dad and Billy and Florrie, his wife, were out one evening, leaving us kids alone. Billy's daughter Norma, would be about fourteen at the time so she was in charge of her sister Joyce and me.

We were playing outside and I fell on a barbed wire fence and tore the upper part of my left arm. I don't remember why I was climbing the fence but I remember the wobbly moment with one leg on top of the wire trying to bring the other past it.

I was all for not telling anyone but the give-away sign of blood on my pyjamas followed by a tearful confession from 'cousin' Joyce gave away our secret. My upper arm had a three-inch tear and proper medical treatment would have involved stitches and antibiotics but Dad regarded these incidents as part of growing up and an opportunity for his backwoods (or is it backward?) Boy Scout skills. I became the victim of a daily hot poultice and tight bandage. Bless him though, Dad meant well but, sixty years later, I still have visible scar on my upper left arm.

I wanted to include it as a 'distinguishing feature' on my passport; 'duelling scar on left arm', but I chickened out.

CHAPTER 11

THE KNIFE CARRYING CULTURE OF MY YOUTH

◆●————————————●————————————●◆

As a boy, I was brought up with an 'always carry a knife' attitude.

'Don't forget your knife, Son!' Dad would remind me as I ventured outside. I always had one with me together with a handkerchief, a shilling, a few pennies in case you needed to use a phone box, a piece of string and a whistle. A 'shilling' (worth five pence in today's money) was enough in those days to buy a decent snack

These habits came from the Boy Scout 'Be Prepared' culture and it's an ethos I still carry today. It's no coincidence that a small notice at our front door reads: 'don't forget, your money, door key, phone, bus pass and the 'purpose' of your outing'.

A Swiss Army Knife was the ultimate accessory. This multi-purpose bright-red pocket knife had a range of tools; can opener, scissors, screwdriver, knife blade and a spiky thing to remove stones from horses' hooves. This feature was designed for soldiers in 1890s who needed to prevent their horses going lame. The advertising literature for these knives was aimed at 'outdoor people and adventurers'. Every boy saw himself as an adventurer although I was more of a dreamer. I still am, according to my family, although I see myself as a practical creative visionary. My daughter Lucy, I'm pleased to say, has inherited this admirable quality from me.

A proper Swiss Army pocket knife was a luxury I couldn't afford so my Dad gave me a big silver pocket knife with two blades and the inevitable stone-removing spike that had belonged to my Grandfather in his army days.

In my Boy Scout troop (and before that, cub pack) we would have a pocket knife linked to our belts through clips designed for this purpose.

Sheath knives were all the rage too. The six-inch blade was contained in a leather pouch (sheath) which looped onto the belt in a 'holster' type arrangement. We would practice 'drawing' them like cowboys from the black and white movies of the day. Quite why we felt the need for speed is beyond me now; it's not as if the sapling branch we intended to cut would run away from us if we couldn't produce the knife quickly enough.

In the formal kilted version of our uniform we wore a 'sgian dubh' ('skee-an-doo') knife in our socks. This traditional knife was an ornamental part of highland dress.

A big part of our self-esteem culture was based on the number of knives we had fastened to our belt. I had my official scout sheath knife and my Grandfathers silver pocket knife, plus the decorative knife in my stocking.

'Big Tosh', our troop leader favoured our kilt-based uniform as it empowered him to carry extra knives in his socks. Not for him the 'ornamental' version; an army bayonet was quite common and he would have inserted a cutlass if it was possible.

Lord Baden-Powell, started these trends when he founded the Boy Scout Movement in 1908 based on his experience with young soldiers during the Boer War. Knives were a necessary part of a soldier's uniform. Removing stones from horses' hooves was probably an everyday occurrence for these young men although never for us. We used our knives to cut branches for shelter and campfires and for removing frayed rope ends for re-splicing.

The sheath knife was useful to gut fish for cooking on the camp fire and a possible lingering smell of fish taught us not to put a dirty knife back in its scabbard.

Then, of course, there was the 'woggle-whittling' trend. In the early days of Scouting, the uniform neckerchief scarf was knotted until, in the 1920s the 'woggle' was born. This was a

51

hollowed wood ring that threaded over the neckerchief to hold it together. The standard issue was a simple rope or leather circle but every Scout worth his salt would design and make his own 'woggle'. We would sit for ages at the camp fire whittling at an appropriate piece of branch and burning holes with a fire heated metal poker to make a neckerchief 'woggle'. My stone-removing spike came in handy to help bore the hole. The conventional woggle was like a tube with a single route through it. My 'piece de resistance' was to use a 'Y' shaped branch section to make a three-holed woggle where the neckerchief entered via two separate tunnels (left and right) and both parts emerging from the bottom.

At International Boy Scout camp gatherings, these woggles were potential trading items – although I never parted with mine. I still have five home-made masterpieces which, thanks to my dad's help, became works of art rather than items of apparel. They all have text and dates burned onto the wood surface and then coloured and varnished. Generations to come might not see them in the same light as I do, but they are sentimental pieces of memorabilia to me.

Part of the 'be prepared' philosophy was to ensure you could make contact in an emergency and we learned to carve whistles. I would moisten a three or four inch section of sapling branch (spit was the best lubricant) and after some tapping with my pocket knife handle, the green bark would slide off. A bit of groove carving and sliding the bark back on produced a kind of high pitched dog whistle. Not really much good in an emergency but satisfying nonetheless. It filled in a few hours on a rainy camp day.

If there had been a 'woggle and whistle whittling' badge, I would have qualified with flying colours.

One of our favourite games at Scout camp was called 'splits' which required reasonably accurate knife throwing skills. You faced your opponent with your feet a natural distance apart and took turns to throw the knife into the ground alongside his feet. You missed a turn if the knife didn't stick in the ground or if it was more than twelve inches from one of his feet and not in a line parallel to them. He, your opponent, would then move his foot to that spot.

The aim (!) was to widen your opponent's stance until he couldn't balance or widen his stance. The game was declared null and void if someone needed to go to the medical tent.

Luckily, we learned first aid too!

CHAPTER 12

'BIRDS OF A FEATHER'

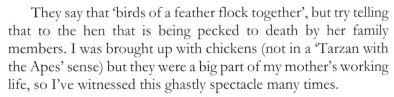

They say that 'birds of a feather flock together', but try telling that to the hen that is being pecked to death by her family members. I was brought up with chickens (not in a 'Tarzan with the Apes' sense) but they were a big part of my mother's working life, so I've witnessed this ghastly spectacle many times.

Shortly after we had moved to Norham, when I was ten years old, Mam started managing the poultry farm of seven thousand (or so) birds. This was the first time I had experienced these creatures as a community and all their clan behaviours.

There is a natural hierarchy and 'pecking order' in a poultry flock and birds that are seen to be different or weak will be victimised. Outsiders, i.e. birds that not of the same 'feather' are like rival gangs and fights will start. Cheeping baby chicks are fluffy and cute, but there's nothing warm and cuddly about adult hens. They are aggressive and will peck to assert dominance and to keep their places in the 'pecking order' and if blood is drawn, the pecking will turn to savage cannibalism. It's not a pleasant sight to see a poor chicken being pecked to death. If spotted in time, my mother would intervene and (mercifully?) wring the suffering creature's neck.

In the movie 'One Flew Over the Cuckoo's Nest', Randle McMurphy (Jack Nicholson's character) compared inmate patient treatment to a "peckin' party"

'The flock gets sight of a spot of blood on some chicken and they all go to peckin' at it, see, till they rip the chicken to shreds, blood and bones and feathers. But usually a couple of the flock gets spotted in the fracas, then it's their turn. And a few more gets spots and gets pecked to death, and more and more. Oh, a peckin' party can wipe out the whole flock in a matter of a few hours, buddy, I seen it. A mighty awesome sight.'

Chicken cannibalism is a serious problem for the poultry and egg production industry and farmers have tried many ways of reducing it. Birds with severe vision problems don't peck others, but blinding the creatures was never considered seriously as a solution. I suspect the practicalities of managing blind hens dominated over any thoughts of humane behaviour towards them.

Chicken 'blinding' spectacles were mass produced in the nineteen-forties and fifties. These glasses were called 'pick guards' that clipped on the beak and blocked forward vision. This reduced the pecking problem as chickens usually only attack the bird directly in front of them. The specs were meant to stay in place but nobody explained this to the hens (anyone who has struggled with clip on nose type reading glasses will understand this).The final version of pick guards had a 'pince-nez' appearance and the promotional literature of the day described how they would make the hen 'look intellectual'. How the marketing people saw that as a selling benefit is beyond me. I can't recall 'Clucky the hen' strutting about in a professorial manner.

According to Wikipedia, on January 16, 1955, Sam Nadler of the National Farm Equipment Company of Brooklyn appeared on, 'what's my line'. The TV show was a popular guessing game, in which a panel attempted to determine the occupation ('line') of a contestant. The audience knew that Mr. Nadler 'sells eyeglasses for chickens' but the panel failed to guess his occupation. Mr. Nadler's identity was revealed to them and he stated that his company sold 2–3 million pairs of chicken eyeglasses per year.

I wish I'd kept some of these red coloured 'pick guards' as, apparently, they are now collector's items.

I came across the Harvard Business School case study 'Optical Distortion Inc' at an IBM training event in 1981. The company designed contact lenses to make chickens see everything in a red glow and not able to distinguish the sight of blood. Most of the students thought the whole thing was a spoof but far from it. It was a solid business based on the premise that the cost of making and inserting lenses was far less than the cost of losing animals to cannibalism. The business case was all very well but it gave no regard to the welfare of the chickens.

'Optical Distortion Inc' lenses were easy to insert but, as any human wearer will testify, can be very uncomfortable if not done sensitively. The business flourished for a while but was hounded by animal welfare groups and came to a halt in 1991.

Like many other poultry farmers at the time, we assumed it would be simpler to adopt the 'debeaking' route. This sounds very drastic but only a small section of beak is burnt off at a few days old so the bird is able pick up food but can't cause serious wound damage as an adult. This process was supposed to be painless and didn't seem to distress the bird unduly, but later studies questioned the 'pain free' theory and the smell of burning bone / skin wasn't very pleasant.

We abandoned that approach and went back to the red pick blinder glasses. Intellectual looking cool 'shades' won the day.

My mother's seven thousand hens were accommodated in an old army dormitory with four enclosed huts where the hens roosted and a central ex canteen and dining area where we cleaned and sorted eggs, kept chicken food and had an incubation pen. I don't know how my mother knew which eggs to incubate. A cockerel was obviously involved somewhere in the process (more than one probably given the number of hens) and I think my mother scanned the eggs under a bright light.

The dormitories were open plan with roosting areas so the hens had room to move around. In later years, the awful concept of battery farming with hens cooped in small cages took over, but my mother had left by then. The poor creatures couldn't peck each other in that environment because they barely had room to turn around. A truly awful approach to chicken farming that should be banned.

Every day, we would clean thousands of eggs (by sanding the surface) and grade them into sizes for vans to collect.

My early efforts to 'help' had eggs shattering all over the electric sanding machine and I had to clean the mess, wipe the machine and change the sanding belt so I quickly had to develop the necessary lightness of touch. We wore masks and had extraction fans to stop us breathing too much eggshell dust.

We would also deliver to local restaurants and pubs. I enjoyed driving round with my mother delivering these eggs. With hindsight, it was probably unwise to let a young man with limited driving experience hurtle round country roads with eggs in the back of a van, but we never had any problems.

Then, of course, there was the time my mother's chickens became movie stars. Maybe it was the 'cool shades' intellectual image of our hen brood that got them selected for a background appearance in 1966 Roman Polanski film. 'Cul de Sac'.

This was a tense thriller filmed at Lindisfarne (Holy Island) about twenty miles away and didn't include any bloody chicken cannibalism scenes as far as I recall. Obviously, no one had mentioned this possibility to Polanski.

The film starred Donald Pleasance, Francoise Dorleac (a rising French actress who, tragically, was killed in a car crash a few years later) and Lionel Stander - and, of course, 'Clucky', our chicken clan leader, and her poultry mates who had put aside differences that would cause them to attack each other and were probably strutting around in the background trying to look intellectual. Maybe we should have let them wear their cool shades. I'll have to watch the movie again to see if there was any 'prima-donna' behaviour from any of them.

I wasn't around when the hens were delivered to the film set and only got to collect them at the 'wrap' so, unlike our hens, I only met film crew workmen and didn't get the chance to meet any of the stars.

That's one up to you, 'Clucky'.

CHAPTER 13

UNWANTED ROAST CHICKENS

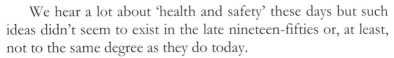

We hear a lot about 'health and safety' these days but such ideas didn't seem to exist in the late nineteen-fifties or, at least, not to the same degree as they do today.

One day, coming home from school, I had spent time in the Harlequin Coffee Bar in downtown Berwick and I missed the 4pm 'school bus' to take me back to Norham.

Actually, I did that a lot, preferring to chat, muck-about, sip frothy coffee with my schoolfriends rather than get a bus full of rowdy schoolkids. I was nervous of rowdy behaviour and 'bullying' towards us Grammar School Boys and preferred to get the 4.30pm 'normal' bus. The school bus conductor (we had them in those days) made no attempt to control the rowdiness and seemed to spend most of his time ogling the pubescent schoolgirls.

One journey home, probably in the late nineteen fifties, we could see flames in the sky as the bus got close to the poultry farm which became very evident as we rounded the corner.

'Let me off the bus,' I yelled at the conductor, 'my mother might be in there!'. Without a murmur from him, or the bus driver, the bus stopped and just let me off.

People were curious and shocked by the flames, but nobody tried to stop me. Nobody asked me what I was going to try to do. Nobody pictured 'schoolboy dies in blaze' headlines or, 'brave schoolboy rescues mother from raging inferno'.

To tell the truth, I didn't know what I was intending to do other than to shout for my mother and pray that she was safe as I ran the hundred yards to get to the location. The bus drove off down the hill into Norham, the village where we lived about half a mile away.

My mother was OK; she told me that fire engines had been called and they soon arrived and started to put out the blaze. The 'poultry farm' (as we called it) was an old army station with four buildings linked to a central reception and entrance area. There were three ex-army sleeping dormitories that housed chickens and what had been a central dining room. It was all very run down and the owner, Jimmy Sommerville (a local farmer, not the singer) bought the place to set up his egg farming business. It was large enough to accommodate eight thousand hens and areas for hatching chicks and for cleaning and packing eggs. There were enclosed pens around the building so the hens could run free during daytime.

One 'dormitory' of hens was lost but the others were fine. There was strong smell of over barbequed chicken, a bit like being inside the kitchen of a KFC shop. Not unpleasant (if that fits with my analogy) until you saw the devastation and burnt corpses inside.

There were lots of wounded and badly burned hens flapping around and Mam was getting to them and wringing their necks to put them out of their misery. That was quite upsetting and it made me cry. Mam too. We did as much tidying up as we could so the remainder of the premises were safe.

The source of the fire had been something electrical, but all of that information went over my head. There wasn't any mystery or wrongdoing, although insurance investigators had a good look around.

The remaining three hen dormitories continued to flourish so life carried on and we collected and processed eggs until the fourth was cleaned out and restocked.

It's a strange coincidence that roast chicken is still one of my favourite meals.

CHAPTER 14

SEGREGATED SEA SWIMMING

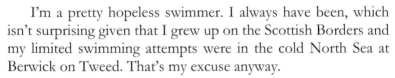

I'm a pretty hopeless swimmer. I always have been, which isn't surprising given that I grew up on the Scottish Borders and my limited swimming attempts were in the cold North Sea at Berwick on Tweed. That's my excuse anyway.

On rare warm summer days, a few brave folks would venture into the River Tweed at Norham, even though we knew about the dangers of its hidden undercurrents. There had been drowning accidents in this river and its neighbour, the more notorious River Till.

'For every yin (one) that the Tweed takes, the Till takes twa' (two)

That traditional saying must be true; it's written in dialect.

Decades later, in the late nineteen-eighties, I was stupid enough to wade in the river Tweed at Norham with my (then) young son Tom on my shoulders and I could feel the tug of the water. Old Patrick, who lived in 'Bridge Cottage' was shouting at me from the north side of the border road bridge - as was Susie. The only redeeming factor about this utterly stupid interlude was that we got to know Patrick (a father Christmas look-alike) and became fans of his watercolour paintings.

But I digress.

Surprisingly, (certainly to me when I think about it), there was a short period in my life when I was keen on swimming. You would find that difficult to believe if you could see me huffing and puffing in the water today.

Swimming, for me, started in the late nineteen fifties at Berwick Grammar School where we had weekly lessons during the summer term.

We swam in the sea (there was no other option) in a tidal pool off the North Sea cliffs about half a mile from the school. There were two of these pools, one designated for women, the other for men.

The segregated pools at Berwick, stemmed from our Victorian ancestors who believed that men and women swimming in close proximity would bring about indecent behaviour. Each gender had allocated separate bathing areas and transgressors could be fined.

The pools were filled by the incoming tide leaving relatively calm, but cold, water. They were about fifty yards apart each with stone built changing facilities.

Female bathing gear of the Victorian era was an unglamorous head to toe smock-like outfit that concealed any view of feminine flesh. Ladies entered the sea from horse-drawn or manually pushed changing huts to avoid being in public view as they entered the water.

Conversely, and partly due to the enforced privacy rules, it was normal for Victorian men to bathe naked.

This gender segregation made life awkward for family groups wanting to enjoy a day together at the seaside and in 1931, mixed bathing became permissible during specified hours. Ladies' costumes maintained their 'cover-all' style.

Our school swimming lessons were scheduled to fit with the tide timetable and during out of school hours, these sea pools were open to the public who, generally, adhered to the established male/female segregation rules.

Albert Ingles, who worked with my Dad, also gave me lessons. He always began by getting me to duck my head completely under the water which I hated and it was many years before I was confident with my head submerged.

I was in my thirties before I plucked up the courage to dive into a pool from the side. Flop head first would be a better description. I still have a school report with the comment, 'Billy has worked hard to learn swimming'. The word 'swimming' flatters me a little – a better description would be anti-drowning.

In 2017, Theresa May, the then British Prime Minister, admitted that running through a grown cornfield was her major act of childhood mischief. Sixty years earlier in 1957 my equivalent wild act was to swim in the ladies' pool with some schoolboy friends. Contrary to rumours, none of us boys grew breasts or lost our paltry manhood symbols. We were, however, rebuked after a diligent passer-by reported us to the school headmaster. A rather limp message about 'respecting accepted conventions, even if you disagree with them' was deemed enough punishment.

A decade later in the late nineteen-sixties we lived in a more relaxed era. Open sea swimming became more popular and the costumes became more fashionable and scantier. The crashing waves provided an ideal background for unashamed skinny dipping, taking us a step beyond the bathing conventions that our Victorian male ancestors had started.

The concept of the 'breast stroke' took on a completely different meaning.

CHAPTER 15

CHRISTMAS TIMES

◆•————————•————————•◆

Like all other young children, I clung to the belief of a reindeer driven bearded fat man flying through the sky to give gifts to all well-behaved kids - and I really mean 'clung'. Most children stop believing at five or six or years old. I was probably eight years old verging on nine. Even when asked, 'Do you still believe in Santa, Billy?', I would say, 'yes', never thinking that the question itself had implications.

This is another example of my 'living in a kind of make-believe, enhanced reality' world. I would stare skyward on Christmas Eve and dismiss my memory of watching Mam stuff presents into a pillow case. These were tough post war late 1940 years, but Mam and Dad's loving generosity meant that I needed something larger than a conventional 'Christmas stocking'. I was probably spoilt, being an only child at the time – and one that nearly didn't get started in life.

I grew up with a fascination of science and things mathematical – like my dad. I would try to rationalise how Santa, single-handedly was able to traverse the world, drop down chimneys and give presents - all in a single night. 'It's a bit longer than that Billy,' Dad would say. 'Given the various time differences, he'll have well over twenty-four hours to do his work'. With my 'wishful-thinking-must-make-it-true' mind, I worked out that that Santa almost thirty hours to do his work. Assuming a billion houses world-wide, with well-behaved children, that makes almost a thousand visits a second. My calculations puzzled me.

'Quantum physics son,' was Dad's standard response, with a knowing nod; 'You'll learn all that stuff at big school later'. That reply worked for me and I would carry on making a hand drawn card to leave in the hearth for Santa, together with a piece of fruit cake (my dad's favourite?) and a carrot for Rudolf. In the meantime, I would watch Mam putting some of my Christmas presents into a pillow case. These, I was told, were the ones that Santa had sent ahead to ease his load. I never questioned the logic of sending a selection of presents ahead. Why not all of them?

'Phew, the sack was heavy this time,' was a typical note that Santa left behind, written in the flowing style very similar to Dad's writing. The fruit cake and carrot would be demolished with only a few crumbs left to add to the realism.

Christmas was a very exciting time; it was a tough job trying to sleep however hard I squeezed my eyes together. I only broke the 'stay in your room until Mam and Dad are up' rule one time. I snuck downstairs (after Santa had left) and opened all of my presents – Meccano box set, Boy's Own Detective book, Dandy Annual, 'Oor Wullie' book (I enjoyed reading). Actually not 'all'. I ignored the more boring handkerchief and sock packages. My attempts at rewrapping didn't fool Mam and Dad but they kept quiet. Either that or my 'acting surprised with every package' was a skill I had perfected. One present would be put aside and given to me a little while after my 'final' package. This was Dad's idea of 'getting over the anti-climax', but his routine became so well known that I expected it.

We continued the Father Christmas myth and ritual with our young children but Susie introduced a bit more logic to the show. Santa brought gifts to be put in bedside hung 'stockings'. Other gifts from friends and family were kept in separate sacks to be opened together after breakfast. These were the decent presents; Santa's stuff was an assortment of novelty bits and pieces together with some biscuits and the inevitable stocking-toe filling Orange. We had two sets of stockings for both of our children, Tom and Lucy, and we would swop the empty one for a full version before we went to bed. Pillowcases reverted back to the uses they were intended for.

The kids still joke about the time when Santa got in a complete muddle. Susie (my wife) and I had got a little too much into the Christmas spirit and we put the children's stockings in the wrong rooms. Lucy, our daughter, got our son Tom's gifts from Santa and vice-versa. Such is the trivia of Santa's stocking content that they didn't seem to mind too much although the following year, Tom pinned a 'this is a boy' notice on his bedroom door. He wanted to catch Santa in the act and his empty stocking would be lashed to his wrist but, luckily, he is a deep sleeper so we would manage to slip it off and replace it with the full version.

I lived out part of my role-playing life when I was asked to play Santa at a local school Saturday event. I had a moustache and beard at the time (auburn) and, taking my fantasy role seriously, I would daub my facial hair with plimsoll whitener. This took a surprisingly long time to wash off and I would rush to my weekly rugby game looking like the grizzled veteran I eventually became.

I had finally got through the 'four stages of Santa'

1. You believe in Santa

2. You don't believe in Santa

3. You become Santa

4. You look like Santa

One year it became my turn to be Santa for our Rugby Club members' children – all of whom are now grown up, many with kids of their own. A few years after me, my rugby playing friend 'Sooty' (as he called himself) played the Santa role. Given that he is a black Ghanaian man proves the power of a child's self-fulfilling belief.

Before we had children, we would run the gauntlet of visiting both sets of parents over the Christmas period. My parents lived near Berwick upon Tweed whilst Susan's family came from Norfolk. We would alternate who got our first visit and overnight stay. There was a lot of driving involved but it worked well. We saw our two families and we also enjoyed two Christmas lunches (a few days apart) and two parcel opening events. We kept to this ritual for quite a while after we had children but, eventually, we opted to have our events at home and invite parents to join us.

We had one family Christmas at our beach house in Heacham Norfolk, complete with decorated tree and log fire. We had reassured Tom and Lucy that Santa would still find us. A last-minute letter up the chimney made sure of that. One of the main gifts that year was a pair of snow sledges; pink for Lucy and blue for Tom (no stereotyping there!).

There wasn't any Christmas snow but tobogganing (to call it by its proper name) works equally well on sand dunes. It was very hard work for us parents though. 'Pull me again, Daddy!'. That's the year we should have bought kites. In my childhood up North, Christmas snow was more regular than not and singing, 'I'm dreaming of a White Christmas' wasn't the fantasy it is today.

Traditionally we have a dinner on 23rd December for friends. This isn't a huge event (fourteen people typically) but it's large enough given our limited sitting and dining room space.

Over the years, our dinner party has established a reputation with people almost clamouring to be on our invitation list and to enjoy our evening with all the fun and games involved. Getting everyone seated around the dining table means that I have to extend it by adding a homemade top to a smaller table. This has worked well over the years until my son Tom took the small table to his house and I had to modify my chipboard top to fit on a different small table.

'Shall we ask Michael to do this?'. Susie was always trying to get a 'proper chap' to usurp my handyman position in the household. She described such a person as being 'a man with a toolbox who knows how to use it'.

This table modifying task would take a competent trades-person no more than an hour. I planned the job very carefully, double checking everything, and by the end of the day had completed the task. It was a fine piece of work and I pondered, during my three of four tea breaks, if I could make a living as a carpenter / handyman. I suspect that's my mind daydreaming again.

Our 'secret Santa' game has become quite notorious and a platform for me to indulge myself and show off. Everyone brings an inexpensive gift. We provide some good ones, together with a few joke presents – a tin of Spam, a roll of black pudding. There's a regular (and awful) Katie Price autobiography that kept coming back. I've since introduced a new rule that presents won cannot return as gifts the following year. People ignore this, of course.

These wrapped gifts are randomly allocated and then opened so everyone can see what's on offer. Then the dice throwing fun starts. I have a special large rubber dice and a board that displays the 'rules' of the game. Depending on the result of your throw, you will be required to 'swop a gift on your left / right', 'take a gift left / right', 'give a gift left / right', 'take from anywhere' or perhaps 'miss a turn'. These aren't options, they are firm instructions. If you have run out of gifts you swop your non-existent package for a real one if required to do so.

We have a 'must take home' rule; you can't leave anything behind and, despite my ruling, I expect to get the Katie Price book back again the following year.

There are a couple of unopened gifts that we throw into the mix. These are surprises and no-none knows what the packages contain (except us). One large ornate box might have a small jar of pickle. Another will have a bottle of malt whisky. Or am I doing a double-bluff with two desirable presents? It's a gamble when you 'blind swop' a nice gift in the hope of something better.

Our children, Tom and Lucy, are now of an age where they like to come to this event so, gradually, our friends are being forced to drop out. I've toyed with building a home extension (with 'proper chaps' to do the job) but it's a lot of money just to accommodate our quirky style of Christmas dinner party.

There'll come a time when our children will want Christmases in their own homes and start to create their own rituals. Susie and I will do our duty and join them. But there'll also come a day when we have Christmas on our own without such rituals.

I can't say I look forward to that totally. On the one hand we'll have peace and quiet and a free choice as to what we do but, on the other, I'll miss my fantasy moments as the world's best secret Santa game-show host and DIY table extension builder.

CHAPTER 16
MY UNAPPRECIATED HOME TOWN

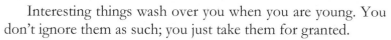

Interesting things wash over you when you are young. You don't ignore them as such; you just take them for granted.

My home town of Berwick-upon-Tweed fits in this category. This fortified town sits in its own county borough on the north east coast, just south of the England / Scotland border. The area is crammed with vivid history and wonderful scenery though to me, it was where I went to Grammar School from age eleven to eighteen. Second to my studying (and sometimes not) my main focus was trying to establish myself as a cool teenager.

History books (unread by me at that time) tell us that defensive walls around the town were first built during the thirteenth century when Edward I took Berwick from the Scots. These fortifications were modernised in the fifteen-sixties by Elizabeth I, who was fearful of the 'Auld Alliance' between Scotland and France.

I would walk through a fortification arch in the town battlements to get to the school which was close to an observation tower where soldiers would watch for enemies. Berwick upon Tweed railway station is virtually next door to the school and on the site of the remains of the town castle. The town changed hands several times until Richard of Gloucester took it for England in 1482.

Locals tell tales of how an administrative error omitted Berwick from the post Crimean war peace treaties, theoretically leaving it at war with Russia until, according to local lore, a visiting Soviet official signed a peace treaty in 1960. The Mayor at the time declared, somewhat tongue in cheek, that 'the Russians can now sleep easy in their beds'.

OK, that's the end of my travelogue.

Like most teenagers, I took this history for granted and was driven more by the desire to conform to the clothes fashions of the day. This was a difficult task not only due to my shyness and lack of confidence but also as my father was suspicious of narrow trousers and 'unconventional' haircuts. My attempts at developing my 'Tony Curtis' quiff in my hair were frowned upon, although I managed to get a local tailor to narrow my school flannels to sixteen inches.

I think it was the American influences that my dad was against. 'Sloppy Joe' sweaters, as he called them, were untidy. I got over this problem by wearing my 'V neck' pullover back to front so it looked like a fashionable crew neck - the downside was that I couldn't take off my school blazer. Looking cool while sweating wasn't always easy.

After school, a few of us would convene in the Harlequin coffee bar next to the town clock tower to drink frothy coffee from pastel-coloured Bakelite cups and sit at Bakelite tables.

Can you name a place where football matches are played in a moat? Trick question, of course. The answer is at Berwick-on-Tweed alongside the Elizabethan defences although the 'moat' had been filled in. The pitch, named 'the Stanks' (a slang Scottish words meaning 'swampy place') had been the home of charity football matches since the early nineteen-hundreds. One side of the pitch ran alongside the defence wall and some spectator 'seats' peered over the drop and had an impeded view of the pitch. The small crowd would stand and cheer and swell forward a little but, thankfully, there's no record of anyone tumbling over the fifteen foot (or so) drop.

Probably the most famous Berwick visitor was L.S.Lowry (the 'matchstick men painter') who was a football fan and one of his sketches featured a Stanks football match.

Lowry was a regular visitor from mid-1930's until his death in 1976. He had been advised to get some sea-air and regarded Berwick as a second home. He produced more than twenty paintings and drawings of Berwick during his visits. There is an official 'Lowry trail' around the town fortifications that follows the footsteps of the great 'matchstick men' painter and highlights the views that he painted.

He always stayed at the 'Castle Hotel' and local residents suspect an equal allure was his unrequited attraction towards the receptionist Marjory Ellison. In a 1961 interview she confessed that she threw away several of his sketches that he had given her, not imagining that he would become famous.

I bet she's kicking herself now.

Lowry might have endured unrequited love in Berwick but so did many others, including me. The town walls that feature in his painting were popular strolling and canoodling place where I failed in my romantic adventures with Margaret Smart. Sorry Margaret, I was probably a little backward for you and now it's too late; I'm a happily married man.

My schoolfriend Peter Davidson and I would roam around the town most Saturday evenings on a bit of a pub crawl before we settled into the regular dance at the Kings Arms Hotel. We'd start at the top of the town at 'The Pilot' Inn, then make our way back via 'The Georgian' pub, the 'Brown Bear' and, finally, 'The Kings Arms'. The Georgian pub was managed by Mr and Mrs Young who had a daughter Christine that our schoolfriend David Rhind was dating. The Young family went on to manage 'The Elizabethan' pub at the top of the town, so our routine changed after that time.

David married Christine and made quite a career for himself as a professor and expert in various geological fields.

Somebody had to.

Eric Lomax was another famous Berwick resident. His time as a Japanese prisoner of war was captured in the film 'The Railway Man' where he was played by Colin Firth. Some of the scenes were filmed in Berwick and the production company organised a 'premier' there.

The local audience were critical with a scene that showed Eric / Colin walking to the town railway station via a cinematically colourful route instead of the real one which meandered down dull looking side streets.

The concept of artistic licence had finally arrived at Berwick on Tweed.

CHAPTER 17

THE AIRD FAMILY

For some reason the Aird family comes to mind whenever I think of my hometown of Berwick on Tweed. I remember Jack, the father, who started cutting my hair when I was eight years old. I was too small to sit on the chair normally so I knelt with my back to the mirror facing the row of people waiting for a haircut. I enjoyed going to a 'proper' barber at last, having graduated from the efforts of a local farm worker who came to our house to do this job. I can remember the hair clippers he used; a device with a lawn-mower like front with blades that went back and forth as the handles were gripped and released, making a 'snick' sound. Maybe that's why we called them snickers. I would sit with a pudding basin on my head and the level of the rim showed where the snicking had to stop. It was crude but effective and I my unruly mop of hair remained intact on top of my head. Now, sadly departed (the mop of hair, not the top of my head).

Barber Jack Aird had a son, also called Jack, so there was 'old Jack' and 'young Jack' and both cut hair.

Old Jack was very friendly and had a line in conversation that never varied. 'Where do you live son?' and after I told him (again) that I lived in Norham (a sleepy village nearby), he would reply.

'Ah yes, Norham, isn't that where the ducks fly backwards?' and he would tweak my nose and say, 'quack, quack'.

This was quite an amusing joke the first few times I heard it but his excuse to tweak my nose stopped after I started to quickly reply, 'I live in Norham, that's where the ducks fly backwards, quack, quack'.

Kneeling on the chair meant that I was facing customers as they came and went. There was a small kiosk at the shop entrance and from time to time, a man would stand in the outer doorway behind the queue of people waiting for a haircut and nod his head towards the kiosk. Old Jack, and sometimes, young Jack would then pause cutting hair and go to serve him. I later learned that the men were buying the traditional three shillings and ninepence 'packet of three' Durex condoms. Dispensing machines of any kind didn't exist in those days. It was usual for Jack (either) to ask 'anything for the weekend' after they had cut hair.

I was never asked this question; the only one I ever had to answer concerned the direction of duck flying.

In more recent years, I bumped into 'young Jack' who was then a widower and had moved into a small cottage in Norham, where my sister lived. I say 'recent years' but this would be in the early part of this century and he would be in his eighties by then. We would chat and reminisce about the old days every time I visited the area until he passed away in 2012.

Another Aird son called Syd, a younger brother to 'young Jack', worked as the projectionist at the local Berwick Cinema, glamorously advertising itself as 'The Theatre'.

We would look back at the flickering projection window to see if we could spot Syd and he would give a little wave if he saw us. It seemed to me to be the most enviable job in the world as you got to see a lot of free movies. I sat in the projection room one time with Syd and a couple of friends. Movie reels were very large and a film, very often, needed several changes of reel so a second, and sometimes third, projector had to be loaded and standing by. Some very long films had an official intermission to allow changeover and to give a comfort break to the audience. This was also the moment when the ice cream lady would wobble backwards down the centre aisle with her flashlight and a smile as frozen as her tray of goodies

After my projection booth visit, I could see that the job wasn't the fun I had anticipated. You didn't get a great view of the movie and you had to be ready to switch projectors and to spot if the film had slipped or even snapped (which was quite a common occurrence). Syd was quite relaxed about this. 'If something isn't right, they'll shout and let you know pretty quickly'. He would shove his grinning face through the projection hole and tell people to calm down with the threat, 'I'm not going to switch the movie back on until you are all quiet and settled.'

Films were very popular in the nineteen fifties and early sixties before television had become established and the town had a second Cinema, 'The Playhouse'. They were equally grubby locations with faded (and dirty) red chintz seating. Very popular though; I can remember full houses for Elvis Presley films (complete with screaming girls) and for a movie titled 'Darby O Gill and the Little People' featuring a young Sean Connery and for 'The Glenn Miller Story', my favourite that I sat through twice – with my neatly trimmed hair and my barber's bother manning the projector.

All now ancient history. Reel-based movie systems were phased out and replaced by digital projectors that could be switched on and off by any cinema employee without specialist skills.

Just as well I didn't pursue that career.

Not that Dad would have let me.

CHAPTER 18

'SCOUTING FOR BOYS'

That's the title of Lord Baden-Powell's book explaining the woodcraft and survival skills that he used in his Boer war days and became his handbook for the Boy Scout movement he founded in 1908. B-P's idea was that young boys would learn useful practical skills and develop sound character.

I am the obvious tribute to his success – although I never gained my 'modesty' badge.

I had three successful years with 5th Berwick Cubs (the group for younger kids based on similar principles), where I rose to rank of Senior Sixer. That meant I got three stars on my, sadly now missing, green cub cap and I was the senior cub. I wasn't as powerful as 'Akela', the lady that ran our group, but I could call the boys to order. Funnily enough, in this environment, the boys accepted my position above them in the pecking order, but less so in the real world!

As I outgrew cub age at eleven years old, I moved up to the 5th Berwick Scout troop, which became my main out of school activity until I was fifteen or so. Dad was keen on the outdoor and 'back to nature' emphasis of Scouting and had rejected the 'boys brigade' route for me as it was too militaristic and army-like.

Nevertheless, we took part in quite a few marching parades wearing our kilt-based uniforms. I remember standing as part of a guard of honour for Her Majesty the Queen's visit to Berwick in 1956; we lined each side of the street and stood to attention as the Queen and her entourage drove past a little too quickly for us to notice anything other than a flash of salmon coloured coat and waving arm.

I still have my original kilt but, unlike in my scouting days where the kilt would wrap around me the regular one and three-quarter times, today it would be a struggle to wrap around once and be secure. It's the genuine article, heavy and worth some money, so I'll leave those that follow to decide its fate, together with that of my sporran and knee length socks.

I transferred from the 5th Berwick troop to 1st Berwick, which sounds like a promotion but only meant that I joined the Grammar School troop.

Most of the activities at our weekly meetings were preparation for camping, erecting tents, tying knots, investigating nature and playing observation-based tracking games. The most useful tracking sign was chalk, stone or twig circle with a stone at the centre, meaning 'gone home'. In B-P's army world, this was a secret signal to inform advancing soldiers that the advanced party of scouts had returned to base or, in our case, it meant that we had stopped playing and had returned to the scout hut.

We also practised semaphore flag signalling (which I can probably still do); a useful skill if I get trapped with a set of semaphore flags and need to send a message. We started / finished our weekly Scout sessions by raising / lowering the flag and saying the Lord's Prayer.

We travelled to Scout camp in the back of Ralph Holmes's fish lorry. Ralph was the County Commissioner and had a splendid uniform to lead our ceremonial parades.

We never went very far for our camping weeks – twenty or thirty miles and we pitched our tents in a designated field. These weren't official campsites like you see today; there weren't any showers or toilet facilities so we had to create everything we needed.

We'd pitch our tents in a neatly spaced row; each one accommodating a 'patrol' (a group of six). The Scout leaders had their own tents and there was a supplies tent for our food and other materials. Some people would be allocated to dig the lavatory (latrine trench) whilst others built the camp 'kitchen'. There'd be a camp fire area at the centre for our cooking and trunks of wood set around it for us to sit. Every patrol (tent) had a 'mug tree'; a branch with strong shoots where we could hang our enamel mugs. Nowadays you buy these mugs with dents already added.

The patrol leader, traditionally, slept by the entrance to the tent. This was legacy from Baden-Powell's army days, when decisions and actions were needed in an emergency. The only emergencies we had was when someone in the depth of the tent needed to rush to the latrines so we positioned habitual offenders at the front. To hell with tradition.

The tent could get untidy and smelly from unwashed teenager body odour so, every morning we had kit inspection. Each gathering of tent occupants ('patrol') stood outside with their kit laid out in a prescribed fashion. We also raised the tent side flaps to let in air to fumigate our sleeping area. We would then repack our kit into our rucksacks before moving it back inside.

The ground was hard and we lay on a waterproof groundsheet. We'd dig a hole in the ground to accommodate our hips when sleeping on our sides. Some boys could live out all sorts of fantasies when sleeping face down.

Part of every Scout's kit would include an army style 'dixie' (portable plate and bowl), and a metal cutlery set that clipped together.

Everything, including the cooking pots for our morning porridge and evening stew was washed in the stream (camp locations were chosen with a nearby stream available for fun and for domestic chores). Fierce rubbing with mud and gravel in the cold water would remove cooking dirt and grease. I don't remember hot water or detergent being used.

Our behaviour was ecological in line with the customs of the day; we dug our lavatories to recycle our waste and, at the end of camp, we unblocked streams that we had temporarily dammed. The policy of 'bash, burn and bury' our empty food tins wouldn't be seen today as the best way of recycling the metal.

First timers at camp had to endure various initiations, a mud covered ducking in the stream and the 'all join hands and touch the electric fence' ritual. Funny how some boys would struggle to be in the middle of the chain thinking they wouldn't get a shock. Obviously not paying full attention in Physics class.

My woodcraft, rope splicing, knotting and axemanship skills helped a group of us win the 'Camping Cup' at a regional Scout event. I can't claim full credit as others were involved too, but I won the key events – axemanship and semaphore. I have the trophy at home (impressively labelled 'camping cup'). I'm not sure how I ended up keeping it and my family will attest that I rarely brag about it (even though I have good cause and haven't won much else!). Other factors that swung this highly prestigious trophy our way was sleeping a night in our home built branch and leaves shelter and cooking a trout without a pan (by wrapping it in leaves and burying it under our fire).

I would call on these skills again in later years in the Spring of 1962 when camping with two schoolfriends, Peter Davidson and George Benton. Going a stage further, we 'tickled' trout in a fast running shallow stream. The fish would doze in the sun (that what it seemed like) and we could submerge our hands gently a few feet from them. Instead of tickling the trout (whatever that meant), we would slowly get our wide-open hands underneath and fling the unsuspecting creature onto the land. Our technique was crude but effective and required both skill and patience.

Our finest achievement on that outing was saving a life. At least that's what we believed. A young boy scout, cold and very tired, stumbled into our field. He was disoriented and dehydrated - and lost from his group. We calmed him, warmed him, gave him some water and freshly cooked trout. He was comfortable and stable by the time his colleagues found him. Peter, George and I remember that as 'the day we saved a boy's life'. Probably an exaggeration but also possibly true.

My Scouting career pinnacle was being part of a Berwickshire group attending an International Jamboree at Blair

Atholl in Scotland. There were Scouts from all over world. I loaned a warm jumper to a Ghanaian scout who was struggling with our climate and I remember 'Bucky' the solo American scout representative who, according to first-time tradition, was instructed to wear his kilt back to front. A very nice guy and a good sport.

My two other highlights were that I had to have a back tooth removed by a local dentist. I had developed an abscess that required a greater level of treatment than the camp dentist could deal with. The town dentist, wearing a dinner jacket (due to an event he was going to, not because he was seeing me) extracted it.

My other highlight (actually lowlight) was that a I failed my first aider badge. A very rude and grumpy Scouter, who was the camp doctor (not my dentist ally) summarised my resuscitation performance as 'terrible, you'll end up killing your patient!'.

Sadly, I failed on that occasion.

CHAPTER 19

NORHAM

◆•————————————•—————————————•◆

Google 'Norham' and you'll discover that this is the name of a charming village in North Northumberland, on the south side of the river Tweed bordering England and Scotland. Norham Castle (of 'Marmion' by Sir Walter Scott fame) was built in the early part of the twelfth century as a bastion of defence for wars between England and Scotland. To continue my travelogue for a moment, the village also boasts a village cross, village hall, central green, two pubs, a few shops and a local primary school. At least, that's how it was when I went to school. The school limps along, some shops have closed and the pub future looks a bit bleak. Nevertheless; it's still a very charming village that my parents loved and Joyce, my sister, has lived there since she was one year old.

We moved from Berrington Farm in 1955 to a council house in St Cuthbert's Square which our parents subsequentially purchased many years later via Margaret Thatcher's 'right to buy' policy.

In the late nineteen fifties, Mam and Dad were keen to buy a village house that was coming up for auction. It was along the 'back lane' of the village with a long garden stretching towards the river. On sale day, Mam fell foul of our butcher of a dentist and needed surgery to remove the stumps of broken teeth, so she missed the auction. I think the house sold for three hundred pounds, which we could have afforded, but that's 'sliding doors' for you.

My sister Joyce had a house nearby in the village and was a great support to Mam and Dad in their later years. After a bit of legal jiggery-pokery (swopping houses) to minimise our mother's care fees, Joyce now owns our original family home and has made quite a few modifications to it. She is happily ensconced there with her partner Paul - and a never-ending supply of Labrador dogs (but only one at a time, I hasten to add)

Dad was proud of Norham and he worked on various committees to promote functions and to raise funds. He was a driving force in getting the council involved in repairing local pathways and walkways.

As a kid, I enjoyed cycling, especially with a folded Woodbine (cigarette) packet inserted between the wheel spokes which, to my ears, made an 'engine sound' similar to a small motorcycle.

Our village policeman, Inspector Stewart, lived in a big house (complete with a gaol) on our main street. One time he caught me riding my bike on the pavement and gave me a stern lecture, threatening me with juvenile court. How times have changed! Perhaps his ears were like mine and my cigarette-packet engine sound made him think I had been riding a motorbike. At the time he stopped me, there wasn't a pedestrian in sight nor a car on the road. Still, rules are rules. Or they were in those days.

Daily life was, I expect, very quiet for our local bobby, apart from the day when a neighbour donned a mask and robbed a rent collector. He worked in the local bakery which gave the Berwick newspaper a dream headline, 'Norham baker runs short of dough'. Our robber neighbour duly served time in prison; he was decent family man but had got into financial difficulties. The village was very supportive.

On Saturday morning, I would be sent to the local shop to get our 'weekly messages' (shopping). I would stand at the counter and pass over my list (my mother's list, actually) to the lady behind the counter who would gather my items and put them in my mother's wicker basket. The concept of self-service hadn't been invented and any such attempted action would be interpreted as theft.

At Willie Morgan's grocery shop you could pop in and buy a 'nip' for sixpence (about 2.5 pence today). This got a small glass of cider that we would pretend was whisky. Not a bad ploy that;

Willie would greet us kids with, 'fancy a nip?' and earn two hundred percent mark-up on his bottle of cider.

The road bridge across the River Tweed marks the border and has the typical 'Welcome to Scotland / England' signs at appropriate ends. For a while, my grandfather (mother's father) lived in the one-bedroomed stone cottage on the Scottish side of the bridge.

In later years, the tenant was Patrick Barclay, a professional artist and son of the artist John Rankine Barclay. Patrick's ruddy face and white beard made him look like Father Christmas; he was a great friend to my young children who loved visiting him. I have four of his watercolour paintings hanging at home. Joyce has a few too; she kept a watchful eye on Patrick and was his unofficial carer and, subsequently, executor of his will.

Dad's fastidiousness and pride in our village is summed-up in the story of when he caught a delivery driver throwing empty cigarette packet from his van window as he drove away. Dad posted this piece of offensive litter to the company head office with a terse note; 'Your driver didn't want this − nor does our village!'

Typical of his public-spirited behaviour.

CHAPTER 20

CARTOONS AND CARTOONING

All through my life, I've enjoyed drawing, painting and cartooning. There are days when I put in bursts of efforts and months when I do nothing. There's something dogged and obsessive about me, but there's also something lazy. I recognise this characteristic and, I suspect, others do too. Especially members of my family,

My school art teacher, Eric Huntley (1927 – 1992) gave me the bug. It was his enthusiasm (he described himself as a 'paintaholic') that made me insist on doing my art 'O' level exam even though I was on the Advanced level maths and physics route.

Dad was a good pen and pencil artist and his talent passed on to me - at least some of it. A lot of it passed through me, settled with Lucy where it has been enhanced.

I enjoy drawing cartoons. I had quite a few published in insignificant magazines, many of which went bust, before having success in some of the glossy periodicals that you could see W.H.Smith.

The pinnacle of my cartooning career was to land one in Private Eye. Issue 1359, 7th February 2014 to be precise and, yes, I have a few copies. Richard Ingrams, during his time as Oldie editor, took a dozen or so of my cartoons during his tenure (he rejected a fair number too but always with the kindly, 'Sorry, not this time' post-it-note).

The last three editions of The Oldie Cartoon book feature two of mine. I have those on my shelf too. More than one copy, actually, with appropriate pages marked

As a kid, I enjoyed cartoon comics and would spend my pocket money on 'The Beano', 'The Dandy' and a few others. But the 'Eagle' comic has stood the test of time with me.

'Dan Dare, Pilot of the Future' was the lead strip cartoon story on the first two pages of the 'Eagle' and he is my favourite cartoon character of all time. Actually, not probably but certainly. 'Eagle' was started by Reverend Marcus Morris, a vicar, who was keen to produce a wholesome periodical that would attract young boys away from the gruesome blood and guts, war based, American comics.

The first Eagle comic issue was launched on 14th April 1950 - I've just checked that by looking at an original framed copy hanging on my study wall; (note to my descendants, this comic is worth a bit of money!).

The Reverend Marcus Morris intended for 'Chaplain Dan Dare of the Interplanetary Patrol' to be the lead character and the original draft drawings had this version. The Fleet Street publishers (Hulton Press) thought this style was a bit 'preachy' and not commercially attractive, so Dan's blue religious uniform was replaced with the green international spacefleet garb. And the rest, as they say, is history.

I have a framed print of the original Chaplain Dan version.

Eagle comic fans (and those that listened to the 'Dan Dare' stories on radio) will know of Dan's adventures, alongside his batman Digby, Sir Hubert Guest, Professor Peabody, Sondar etc. and how they would protect humanity from the evil Mekon and his Treen army.

At Berrington farm, I'd be about six years old when, after a tiff with my parents, I put my dressing gown over my pyjamas and said I was leaving home. I can't recall what had upset me. They both laughed when I packed my small suitcase with Eagle comics (nothing else) and set off. Their laughter made me angry but I'd only gone a few steps when Mam asked if I would like to start my journey with a mug of cocoa and a cake. Dad commented that people might steal my comics and 'wouldn't it be better to stay home for now?'

A face saving solution for all of us!

There were lots of other good characters in the Eagle at least one of which was sponsored.

The cartoon strip title read: 'Walls Ice Cream presents TOMMY WALLS The Wonder Boy'. In each story, Tommy (probably the first UK comic superhero) would solve dastardly crimes. At a vital moment he would eat an ice cream for energy ('Walls' naturally) and after making the lucky 'W' sign with his fingers and thumbs, he would instantly transform into his action super-hero.

I liked the lucky 'W' sign as it reflected my name and would do it quite a lot in my imaginative play. I don't do it now of course – at least not very often and not where I can be seen.

Later issues of Eagle featured 'Luck of the Legion', a story of a band of French Legionnaires. This too was a sponsored feature, this time by 'Eat Me' dates and I can remember getting a French legionnaire 'kepi hat' by sending six date packet labels and a 1/6d (about seven pence today) postal order.

I loved the 'PC 49' and 'Riders of the Range' characters and have a couple of strip cartoon books, but Dan was always my favourite. He behaved with impeccable honour and decency and, even in the toughest of circumstances, would never break the rules of 'fair play'. "No Digby, we must keep our word."

There's a cartoon panel in the 27th July 1951 issue picturing Dan saluting a colleague who sacrificed his life to destroy a humanity-threatening weapon. Dan is drawn standing to attention and saluting with the thought bubble 'thanks Old Timer – your planet won't forget'. It made me cry all those years ago and makes my eyes prick a little today when I look at it.

Hawk Books published fourteen large hardback annuals containing the first ten years of Dan Dare stories. These were the best years before later publishing companies made 'modern modifications' to the Eagle. I have all of these (plus a few spares). These would my 'Desert Island Discs' book selection.

Frank Hampson's original Dan Dare art panels are highly sought after and very expensive. His iconic art style and sense of detail broke the cartooning mould of the day and another prized book of mine titled 'The Man Who Drew Tomorrow' summarises his life.

I once owned an original art page from the Dan Dare story in Eagle Annual Number 7 drawn by Desmond Walduck, but I sold it in 2017. This seemed a good idea at the time but it wasn't. I lost money on my original price and I miss not having the drawing; I'd now pay more than double to get it back if I could track it down.

We'll see....

I came to Jeff Hawke cartoons fairly late in life. I knew of these Daily Express comic strip stories but it was only after I met, and became friendly with, the artist Sydney Jordan ten or so years ago that I started to buy some originals. I have eight of these hanging on my wall, two of which were presents from Sydney. We meet every year at the 'Jeff Hawke Club' reunion and long may this continue.

I had a go at creating a Dan Dare artboard as part of post heart surgery recuperation in 2016.

It's not too bad but both Frank Hampson and Sydney Jordan still retain their laurels.

CHAPTER 21

HOLIDAYS BEFORE PACKAGES

◆•————————————•————————————•◆

Up to my late teenage years, the word 'holiday' to me just meant a break from going to school. Concepts like 'holiday packages' and 'travel agents' didn't exist in those days – at least not to my family.

For me, going on holiday (I not sure we even used that phrase) would mean two weeks summer camp with the Boy Scout troop - or a camping weekend with friends.

I don't remember my parents going on holiday, other than when we packed the car to go and stay with relatives - often less than a couple of hundred miles away. Relatives would come and stay with us too – sometimes unannounced; that was their 'holiday'.

The family we visited most was the Ingledew family. These were wartime friends of my parents and 'Uncle Billy' (as we called him) was best man at their wedding. He was in the RAF and lived in army housing and was transferred from place to place every few years.

In 'Uncle Billy', you would never meet a more unlikely airman; he didn't fly a plane (he couldn't even drive a car) and he was totally unpractical so I assume he had an administrative job. He was a wonderful piano player and in his later years (as a widower) wandered off to Spain to play music in bars. A great character – he almost deserves a Chapter of his own!

His daughters (my 'cousins' as I referred to them), Norma and Joyce were around my age (Norma a few years older) and both great fun. All sadly now passed away, but never forgotten.

Dad had a ritual for packing the car for our two hundred mile journey; he was precise and would plan to handle every possible emergency situation. "It's called contingency planning son; you never know what could happen"

I think I might have inherited some of his fastidious planning habits.

In Dad's defence, cars were not as reliable as they are today; they didn't have dashboard lights to highlight a problem. The acronym 'POWER' was key to his checklist; petrol, oil, water, electricity (battery) and rubber (tyres). We never went anywhere in the car without a 'power' check-up. Does anyone do these checks nowadays or do they expect the car to self-diagnose a problem? I certainly do! (sorry Dad, changing times).

We were members of the 'Automobile Association' (AA) and had the iconic metal badge displayed on our front bumper. This British motorist friendly association was founded in 1905 and offered all aspects of help to the British driver. In those days, the AA man travelled the roads on a motorbike and sidecar and wore an army style Khaki uniform. The yellow sidecar was a repository for tools, spares, maps and a first-aid kit. These drivers seemed quite plentiful and each one had a 'territory' he would patrol. At various points along the main roads and at junctions, there were AA telephone boxes and every association member had a key so he could open it and call for assistance. There was something magical about these distinctive looking blue boxes.

Every time an AA motorcycle driver spotted the association badge on a car, his right arm would shoot up into a crisp military style salute. Dad would wave in acknowledgement and I would return an equally crisp salute. Rumour has it that, in their role as the motorists' friend, the AA man didn't salute when there was a police speed trap ahead.

Around the late nineteen fifties, the 'powers that be' stopped these men saluting on the grounds of safety (and to stop them warning about police speed traps).

Any journey over a hundred miles (such as travelling to Yorkshire to stay with relatives) was a huge adventure. It involved several stops by the side of the road to brew up cups of tea, eat our pre-packed sandwiches and to study nature. There weren't convenient cafes or hotels (at least not within Dad's budget or inclination) and quite often we had to camp out at night. Thankfully by then we had a dormobile van that we could sleep in – or, at least, some of us could.

My other holidays were organised school trips; a geology trip to Yorkshire, staying in a hostel, a trip to Paris in 1959 and a 1962 trip to Switzerland. We travelled by train and coach; flying wasn't seen as a viable option as relevant airports were too far away and it would be too expensive for many of us anyway.

These trips were my first ventures abroad (although I used to think of outside Northumberland as being 'abroad'). I didn't fly on a plane until 1969 when I enjoyed a weekend in Majorca with a couple of Aussie rugby playing friends.

I was in my mid-twenties when I went on my first skiing trip to Kitzbuhel Austria with some friends; I recall the fun of the travel as much as the fun of the snow. No flying was involved and we travelled on the 'Snowsport Special'; a train from Waterloo station that had a discotheque and a twenty-four-hour bar. I barely recall the names of my travelling friends; mainly 'Aussies' and a mad dentist (also Australian) called 'Screwy' – I can't recall his proper name.

On one of our rugby playing tours to France, our coach driver ('Brummie' from Birmingham) kept asking, "what does je ne sais pas mean". We would duly answer, "I don't know". "OK", he'd reply, "I'll ask someone else"

Little things amused us then – and him too, obviously.

CHAPTER 22

SPORTING DISASTERS AND DECEPTIONS

◆•─────────────•─────────────•◆

That's quite an off-putting title to summarise my sporting life. I did have some success and I have certainly had lots of enjoyment over my life – mainly at rugby and tennis. More enjoyment than success actually.

The biggest failure was a disaster. Nothing due to me, I might add, and I'm only including it because of its seriousness and its unforgettable nature.

If this incident was a Chapter on its own, I would head it; 'the day I witnessed a schoolteacher killed by a javelin'. I don't recall the teachers name (he wasn't from our school) but I remember the name of the competitor who made the throw. It wouldn't feel right to disclose it, so I'm not going to. It was a freak accident and not the throwers fault.

We were at Shielfield Stadium at Berwick on Tweed (the home of the town football club) for a sports day with some local school participants and a few top UK athletes. I was sitting in the spectator seats with a very clear view. If I were to allocate fault, it would be mainly with the victim (a teacher who wasn't paying attention) and, I suppose, the casual nature of sports safety rules that were prevalent in those days. An exceptional javelin throw caught the victim unaware and left him with a javelin impaled in his head. I can still see the blood on the hands of Harry Bligh, our PE teacher who tried to help (you can't 'unsee' these things). I can recall the commentator, Mr Dawson asking the First Aid people to move quickly; two first aiders were walking towards the accident with obvious nervousness and reluctance. It probably wouldn't have made any difference, but I still get slightly angered at these people. This wasn't a sprained ankle, for God's sake!

An unforgettable sporting incident for all the wrong reasons, sadly. RIP sir.

I wasn't very good at school football or cricket but I enjoyed athletics. I could run quite fast over a short distance so classified myself as a sprinter. I had the spiked running shoes (probably still got them somewhere) and was part of the BGS (Berwick Grammar School) sprint relay squad. I didn't feature as an individual winner in any events.

Our sprint squad raced in the Northumberland schools' finals day at Newcastle. I was the start off sprinter as I seemed to be better at running round the left turn bend than running in a straight line. Maybe one leg is slightly longer than the other or one side is heavier. We used to make the joke that as I 'hung to the left', this extra weight made me a natural bend runner. When I say 'we' used to make the joke, I really mean that 'I' used to make the joke.

An athletics track has six or so lanes and the start points are staggered to balance out the bend and to ensure all teams run the same distance. I started in lane five and there was a gap in lane four as one team was missing. The official at the start position should have put me in lane four as that was where my three other team mates were positioned. I hurtled round the left turn bend, aided by my natural 'hanging to the left' attribute and could see my colleague (David Borthwick) waiting to receive the relay baton in lane four, reducing my running distance by five or six yards. A gradual drift got me there ahead of the other runners (just!) so our sprint relay of 440 yards was probably only 430 yards in total. I think we still came in the last two.

Despite my starring performance to beat other 'starter' relay sprinters, I wasn't approached to be part of the county team. Maybe the officials knew their error and decided to keep it quiet. We didn't win after all.

I'm not sure that my colleagues knew about the lane error but as they kept congratulating me on my great 'first relay leg', I didn't mention it.

As an 'athlete' (with my own set of running spikes), I categorised myself as a triple-jump specialist although in my day, it had the more girly 'hop-step-and jump' title. That describes the mechanics of what happens; you start with a hop (take off and land on same leg). Followed by a step (from one leg to the other) and then a final jump. I was OK at it, not world-beating, but probably the best in Berwick Grammar School. At the same school county sports event where my 'hang-to-the-left' skills featured in the sprint relay, I achieved third place in the H-S-J. Admittedly it wasn't the most popular category of athletics and there weren't too many entries; less than four, in fact.

I took my running spikes with me when I went to Bristol University, imagining that I would become part of the athletics fraternity and for a short while, I trained with Gwynn Morgan-Jones, a young man from Wales who was the British Schools triple jump champion. He was very encouraging and, although my skills improved, I never exposed myself to further competition. I couldn't possibly beat my 'fastest sprint relay start man' and 'hop-step-and-jump' bronze medallist achievements (even though we didn't get medals).

Fate intervened again when I joined the University Freshers Cross Country race. The event was for new University undergraduates ('freshers') and raced across four miles of countryside on Bristol Downs. I couldn't sustain the pace and stay with the pack of almost a hundred runners and, together with my friend David Rhind, got lost near some woods. We took, what seemed to us, the obvious path and emerged on a road behind a small running group so we tagged along and found ourselves finishing the race in the top twenty or so. Despite omitting almost a quarter of the race, we looked pretty knackered and probably how a good top twenty cross-country runner would look.

That was my last competitive athletics event. The running club organisers kept asking me to join other sessions, but I decided to retire on my not totally honest set of laurels. It's a relief to get that off my chest at last.

CHAPTER *23*

EDUCATION AND THE 'SLIDING DOORS' IMPACT

◆————————————●————————————●◆

The phrase 'Sliding Doors' comes from the 1998 movie of the same name and portrays how a chance moment or decision impacts everything that follows. Our lives are all based on the choices and decisions we make, or which are made for us.

The measure of success, in my schooldays, was based on academic achievement at school and University, followed by getting a good job. That was what my parents hoped for and, therefore, that became my ambition too. As far as I was concerned, the 'education system' knew best. 'It' decided that I should take a science-based route and, prior to 'O' level (the exams at sixteen years old), I dropped subjects like History and English Literature so I could take 'O-level' Maths and Science early and move on to the more advanced stuff.

Similarly, I did my French exam a year early so I could tick it off and 'get it out of the way'.

People sometime say 'schools aren't what they used to be'. No, they are not - thank goodness; they are much better today. The well-intentioned decision for me to focus on a narrow range of subjects defined my career options quite a few years before I was mature enough to decide for myself. There's a 'sliding door' scenario if ever there was one.

Things probably wouldn't have turned out any different, but we'll never know. In some parallel universe, I could be complaining about working in a theatrical and arty environment and bemoaning my missed opportunity to have worked in the City.

During out fifth year at Berwick Grammar School, we boys had to decide between pursuing Latin or Woodwork whilst the girls had a Latin versus Domestic Science choice.

No stereotyping there!

I was good at Latin but, following the macho trend, I took the sawdust and glue path like most boys - another 'sliding door' situation. My consolation was that woodwork involved graphical drawing which I was keen to do.

From the regimented restrictions of school, where I felt that the real me didn't quite emerge, I found myself at Bristol University with complete freedom of choice about all aspects of my life. Having complete control over how I spent my time brought too many new challenges and choices for my almost, butterfly-oriented brain.

How could someone who showed huge academic potential at school level, struggle so much and very nearly fail to get a University degree? It was nothing to do with my intellect; it was down to my apparent inability to stay focussed.

'Vivid imagination', 'butterfly mind', 'unfocussed talents' and other, not always flattering phrases, have been said about me throughout my life. All very true - and I'm guilty as charged. I'm still like that today although I try to pass it off as some kind of personality charm.

I had lots of fun and I enjoyed the formality of University; the dinners in Wills Hall where, every weekday evening, we wore jacket, tie and an undergraduate gown. I had one lapse in behaviour; thankfully undetected. One evening dinner, I spun a cork table mat across the room and mayhem followed. Mats flew everywhere, one hitting the Warden at the top table who then walked out in disgust. Not my proudest moment and the 'sliding door' impact could have cut short my University life. Now you've read that, kindly forget it.

I spent two enjoyable years in Will Hall, before moving to a flat with some friends for my final year. In Wills, I had a study / bedroom in the main quadrangle; room N7 – occupied many

95

years later by Derren Brown; I'm sure my residual aura was a 'sliding door' that influenced him.

Hall events, drama groups, balls and various club and society activities absorbed most of my time, leaving little for serious academic study. 'I can catch up later' I thought.

My main subject was 'Physics', chosen because I was good at it at school and because that's where the opened 'sliding door' sent me. My good friend Jumbo was my partner at the hands-on practical sessions, where we would perform structured experiments on various scientific principles. His tendency to nod-off to sleep whilst I was calling out various data led us to retro-fit our measurement data to reach the desired conclusion. Just as good a learning experience.

During my University years, I discovered an attraction towards the opposite sex, generally unrequited and, of course, impeded by my crippling shyness. Drama events helped a lot; the various parts and roles that I played at stage events forced the occasional closeness with ladies and the scripted words gave me temporary confidence.

The October 1962 Cuban missile crisis gave a potential impetus to my love life. President Kennedy's barricade stopping Russian ships bringing nuclear weapons to Cuba put the whole world on edge but my pleas of, "let's not wait, the world could end tomorrow!" to every young lady I met, sadly had no effect. I joined a march in Bristol City centre; not because of the politics, but because I fancied a waitress who was joining it.

The threat of war went away when Krushchev, the Russian President, capitulated. Sadly, for me, my waitress friend didn't.

Inevitably, my many non-academic activities impeded my studies and, after my second year, I was bumped off the 'honours' degree path to try to gain an 'ordinary / pass' version.

My school headteacher, Mr Whitehouse, a perceptive man, foresaw this possibility. I had written to him commenting on my difficulties and fears about failure. He urged me to stick with it, "even 'Professor' Jimmy Edwards (a popular radio comedian of the day)", he told me, "got a degree – of sorts."

Towards the end of my final year, I started to revise furiously. I felt compelled to get this 'degree of sorts' that was expected of me, but even that work had to fit around an Easter holiday show that the University Revue group was performing at Bristol YMCA theatre. More on that in a later chapter.

A good friend of mine, who was also performing in the show, had wangled an extra study year. This seemed a better alternative to getting a proper job so I wrote a letter to my tutor (Dr Thompson) applying to extend my studies.

I am strangely proud of his 'Dear Freeman' reply.

'Dear Freeman,

Any application to stay for a further year's study would be considered by the University board. However, when I look at your record, I note that you have taken twelve examinations of which you have failed five. You have passed six of the remaining seven by the narrowest of possible margins and therefore I see little chance of your request being successful'

He was right.

That' Sliding Door' stayed firmly shut.

CHAPTER 24

MY SPORTING LIFE

The title of this chapter is reminiscent of a movie 'A Sporting Life' that brought the late Richard Harris to fame. It was a gritty tale about a tough northern rugby player. I am from the north and I played rugby but there the similarities end. I did wear a Richard Harris stage costume once, but more on that later.

There are quite a few people that have played rugby for almost thirty years but not many started their playing 'careers' at twenty-one as I did. It was all a coincidence really ('sliding doors'?) as I didn't follow rugby, I hadn't seen many games (one at University, I think) and couldn't claim to have been a fan that always yearned to play the game.

The connection was via an old Berwick friend Robin Stoddard and although he went to a posh boarding school, he mixed and drank with us when he was home. His family owned and ran a couple of pubs and a café in Berwick, so our paths crossed quite a lot during our pub wanderings.

A year after leaving University, I lived in a flat in Holland Road, fairly near Olympia and Barons Court. Robin lived a mile away, in slightly deeper Barons Court, with friends he had picked up along the way. Our watering hole was 'The Cedars' pub where we would sing Irish songs in the back room. Noisy, uninhibited and great fun. We probably went there two or three times a week. As well as the singing (mainly 'Clancy Brothers' Irish songs) one chap would produce a tin whistle and play along and, occasionally, a mouth organ player joined in. I had a hankering for harmonica (proper name for mouth organ) but I did nothing about it. Just image, dear harmonica playing daughter Lucy, how good I would have been if I had started then and not waited over forty years for you to inspire me!

Robin, his friends and the Cedars pub were my entre to Harrodian Club, the sports and social facility for the iconic Knightsbridge store. This was destined to be a focal point of my social life for many subsequent years. That and the drama group that I later joined (thanks to Bill Rodwell, one of my rugby contacts) - and also IBM; I mention that too so I'm not viewed as someone who had a narrow life.

Robin encouraged me to join in the early season rugby training sessions and things started from there. I didn't know much about the game but I coped by just being big and aggressive and I was still reasonably speedy. The club captain at the time was Graham Franklin who, many years later, ran the Churchill Hotel and did us a great favour in helping with the wedding reception for Susie and me.

The Harrodian Club was eventually sold (around 2000) and is now a private school that, at one time, taught the actor Robert Pattinson.

The Knightsbridge store didn't produce many rugby or soccer players so outsiders, like me, were tolerated. It served us well over the years and the facilities were great; we had tennis courts of every type, two squash courts, a small gymnasium and an outdoor swimming pool. Eventually, the status of outside members was formalised and we had full family membership for only fifteen pounds a year. This was my only rugby club (apart from a thriving pub side called the 'Sinners' based around the 'Sun in Splendour' pub at Notting Hill Gate).

My rugby career (!) grew and by the early nineteen-seventies, I was club captain of Sinners RFC for the 1972/73 season and captain of Harrodians the following year. Each week I would telephone the match score to 'The Daily Telegraph' for inclusion in the Sunday scores listings. My mother, bless her, always thought we were doing well as we stayed one place below Harlequins, a top-class club she had heard of. It was a while before she realised (perhaps I told her) that the table was in alphabetic order.

In the days before internet and mobile phones, team members would be 'carded'; a formatted postcard would arrive announcing the team you had been selected for and where the game was to be played. For some of the 'away' games, we would meet at Harrods store in Knightsbridge and board a coach. We were asked to gather at a side entrance so the impact of a gaggle of noisy rugby players with bags (and sometimes cans of beer) didn't disturb the flow of elegant purchasers coming to the store.

A few players (not many) actually worked at Harrods. Andy Dolman ('Mr Dolman' as he was known to his staff) was the head of men's clothing and became a good source of reduced-price suits.

I played for Harrodian club on a Saturday and a few times a year we played as the Sinners Rugby club on a Sunday. Both of these clubs were magnets for Australian visitors; players would return home to Oz and tell their rugby playing friends about these 'bonza clubs' in the UK. I can't be certain that they used those words but I'm trying to capture the spirit of the day! Even though I haven't seen many of these people for decades (and some, sadly, are no longer with us), I regard them as 'lifelong friends' and our conversations, I'm sure, would pick up as if there hadn't been a break.

When I met Susy in 1981, she didn't know very much about rugby but accepted that it was a passion of mine and part of my routine. The only game she had watched was the British Lions playing a test match against the Springboks in South Africa. When we got together, I was playing for Barnes veterans (an evolution of the Harrods team) and I took her along to watch us play our annual grudge match against Battersea Ironsides. A cracking game, as I recall, although Susy wasn't knowledgeable enough to see its qualities.

Our first rugby tour was in 1969 to Limerick where we played the Garryowen Club who had reached the finals of the Munster Cup. They were better than us and we went down 6 – 36 but they agreed we had tested them (in what? I wonder). We were slightly undone by the expert quality of refereeing that stopped us deploying some of our carefully crafted talents. Our referee was a local man Paddy D'Arcy who, one week later, officiated at the Scotland v. England Calcutta Cup match at Twickenham. We fared better in our second game against a local club Abbeyfeale, losing 12 – 14. We should have won comfortably and probably would have if the draught Guinness hadn't taken its toll.

We toured every year (the club still does) but I dropped out in 1982 after our trip to the far east where we played at Happy Valley race course in the centre of Hong Kong. That was my fourteenth and biggest tour and it seemed a good time to call it a day. We had played in Jersey, France, Italy, Holland, Isle of man, Cyprus and had won a plate competition in Florida.

Interspersed in all of these was one Harrodian Club venture to Majorca where we flew Laker Airways. Freddie was on board and I did a filmed interview with him. I must dig out the reel.

We produced a magazine for every trip to raise funds and I found myself as the naked pin-up in one of them; my hands covered sensitive areas and a rugby ball hid my face. I think the idea was that people would have fun guessing the identity of the 'mystery pin-up'. I held myself in readiness for screaming girls to rush up and claim their prize of a night out with the player concerned. I'm still waiting.

The week before my fiftieth birthday (which was on a Saturday), I broke my collar bone. I remember a lady in a waiting room telling her husband (with admiration in her voice);

"Darling, this gentleman got injured playing rugby just before his fiftieth birthday"

I waited for admiring comments and requests for an autograph, but all he said was:

"Stupid C*nt"

A soccer player obviously.

My cricketing moment of fame was at Lords. Not as a player (unsurprisingly) but as a member of the crowd when I leapt in the air and caught a 'six' single handed. My father in law, Leslie, was with me as was Ben, my brother-in-law. I think that's the correct title (he's married to my wife's sister). I'm very grateful for these witnesses as, I'm sure, my story would be viewed as one of my flights of fancy.

It was the summer of 1989 and England were playing Australia. Simon O'Donnell was the batsman and Ian Botham the bowler. Mike Flynn, a rugby character famous for producing the 'Jock Strapp Ensemble' records was sitting two rows behind me in the Mound Stand. He had played rugby for Hampstead and I knew him vaguely. He's no longer with us and, although one shouldn't speak ill of the dead, I had always found him a bit unsufferable. He was the kind of person that considered himself more amusing and entertaining than he really was (who am I to talk!). Mike was in full flow during the cricket and despite the fact that some of the crowd found him amusing, I wished he would shut up and let us enjoy the game.

After my leap to catch the ball, he shouted, "Blimey. If you hadn't have caught that, it would have hit me in the mouth"

Most of the crowd applauded my catch but I'm sure a minority would rather I had let it go.

To be fair to Mike, he gave me a glass of champagne.

CHAPTER 25

HOLIDAY CAMP WORKING

◆•——————————•——————————•◆

I had two summer working sessions at Butlins Holiday amps; 1962 at Filey and 1963 at Minehead. Or possibly the other way round; my memories and experiences have blended into a single event and the few photographs I have don't help. It doesn't matter, the main recollections are clear and the geography isn't important.

Billy Butlin was a South African entrepreneur who transformed British family holidays with his holiday camps. He set the trend of all inclusive, action packed family holidays that have been copied (and improved!) by Mark Warner, Centre Parks and other providers locally and internationally.

He started in 1936 but most of his venues were developed after the Second World War and were built around old army camps. The facilities were simple; chalet type accommodation with bunk beds, often four to a room. Central dining (two sittings), swimming pools, bars and organised entertainment. some of which was the 'happy camper, all join in stuff' that we've seen parodied on tv.

On both occasions I was employed for a six-week period as part of the kitchen and restaurant staff. There were a few regular old-stagers, but most employees were young people, students and what we would call today, itinerant workers. I don't think work applications were rigorously vetted.

The Red Coats were a separate breed. These were the entertainment officers and announcers employed after interviews and auditions to prove they could speak with confidence. They were the front-line staff that mixed with the holiday makers and the heart of how people remember Butlins. They wore red blazers, white trousers / skirts, and white shoes; the dream outfit for a person who enjoyed showing off and I would have loved to have worn it. Many of these redcoats saw themselves as would-be entertainers. The majority of them were pleasant and approachable but a few were aloof and thought themselves worthy of greater things.

Every week a new batch of professional entertainment acts would perform in the evening. Singers, comedians, ventriloquists, jugglers, magicians, this was the era of variety shows. Some visiting performers became famous in later years having started their careers at Butlins; Jimmy Tarbuck, Des O'Connor, Michael Barrymore, Norman Vaughan, Dave Allen, Rod Hull, Terry Scott, The Bachelors, Susan Vaughan. Even Cliff Richard performed at one of the camps before his first hit in 1958. I saw The Batchelors, Susan Vaughan, Arthur Worsley (ventriloquist) and Terry Scott.

Together with my kitchen staff friends, I would mingle with guests trying to impress young ladies by implying that we knew these people well.

My main employment was as 'breakfast kitchen hatchman'; a very unglamorous job. I stood at my allocated 'hatch' area and the waitresses dumped dirty dining plates in front of me. I would scrape the debris from the plates and stack them for washing. Between scrapes I would fill breakfast bowls with prunes, grab toast and pats of butter and jam, ready for the waitresses to take to the diners.

We were given (and had to sign for) a 'hatchman scraping tool'. This was a large plastic spatula designed to scrape the uneaten scraps from the plates but it was quicker to use our hands. A deft backhand scrape with the heel of my left hand and the plate was ready for stacking. But the job didn't finish there, we had to multi-task, so after a quick wipe on my apron I would plunge my hands into the large vat of prunes and emerge with exactly eight pieces, which I deposited in a breakfast bowl.

We 'hatchmen' had this ritual off to a fine art; scrape plate, wipe hands, stack plate, grab eight prunes and deposit them in a breakfast bowl, move the bowl so the waitress could pick it up (wink at waitress)… all repeated at a frantic pace. We were proud of our skills and had an 'aura' (literally) amongst other kitchen staff.

Accidents would happen from time to time, typically a dropped plate which we would kick to one side for the kitchen porters to clear away. In this frantic cycle we made other mistakes too; I recall pouring a jug of cooking oil into the prunes thinking it was prune juice; only one person from about two hundred diners complained that the prunes were greasy.

Tummies were obviously tougher in those days.

It was fun shift work and there was a great camaraderie with the other staff. I took my turn at basic fetching and carrying – plates, utensils and, occasionally, I was in charge of 'Jackson Trolleys'; large heated containers that held plates of food (usually breakfast bacon and eggs) on racks. I would wheel these into the dining room so waiting staff could access the meals.

I developed my early poetic and satirical writing skills at Butlins as, unbeknown to many, I was one of the notorious 'shithouse poets'; an elite bunch of graffiti scribblers that took the p*** about senior Butlins management with words and images daubed and on the lavatory walls. A forerunner to Banksy. For any readers researching this, my penname was 'Mac', there was also 'Ern' and 'Vic' but (like 'Banksy') our identities were secret. If we did little else, our scribblings forced management to have the lavatories cleaned regularly. There were staff notices threatening 'dismissal to the perpetrators' which I took as a compliment to my 'work'

I did other camp jobs to supplement my income; organising kid's games, late night security patrol (the things I saw!) but my favourite part time work was being a member of the chalet allocation crew on Saturday 'change-over' days. Guests who had finished their holiday left after breakfast and new guests would join the camp during the afternoon. I would check them in and, like a hotel, allocate a chalet, give directions and pass over a key. The pay rate wasn't anything to write home about but in a four-hour shift, I could chat to quite a lot of girls and get in a position where I could greet them as a friend at the bar in the evening.

There was occasional banter between registering groups; men would offer me drinks in exchange for getting a chalet near ladies they fancied, or just getting their names - and I would call in these debts later. Personal data protection rules hadn't been invented in those days.

As far as I know, we only had one complaint about accommodation and that came from a woman who (mistakenly) had been allocated a chalet with man she didn't know.

I have no idea how that happened (not on my watch) but it was a Wednesday morning when she asked to be moved.

There's a back-story there!

Happy camper days.

CHAPTER 26

AND HOW IT ALMOST BECAME REAL LIFE

I've 'bigged up' that title. It was never a real possibility that I would abandon my serious corporate life (despite the fact that it didn't really suit me) and become a holiday camp working hippy. I did get the offer though, and a different 'sliding door' decision would have altered my life path from my early thirties.

One evening, drinking in my local pub (the 'Sun in Splendour', Notting Hill Gate) I agreed to join others on a Club Med Holiday. Giles, a rugby playing friend, was intending to go with his chum; a slightly irritating man called Eric and others (also signed-up members of the 'slightly irritating club'). Last minute family reasons ("Giles I'm pregnant!") meant that he dropped out and my friends on this first trip were Nat Bitton, Dick Smythe, Peter Boyd plus 'slightly irritating Eric' and his teammates.

We knew about the straw cabins in the woods, no electricity in sleeping areas ('bring a torch'), the fun, the food and the girls. The anticipation of those last three points wiped out worries about straw cabins and lack of electricity. Late night flashing torchlights as people struggled to find their cabins together with intermittent noises of romantic lovemaking, were all part of the package we had paid for.

I wasn't a hippy by nature but I succumbed to wearing a wrap-around loincloth, interspersed with my blue djellaba (kaftan). I can still wriggle into it, but family pressures mean that I rarely do so.

I shared a hut with my big friend Nat and we were content with the simple, yet comfortable, accommodation of a couple of beds, some hanging space and a door that closed with a 'not-always-easy-to-find' hook.

Necklaces of coloured beads acted as currency for bar drinks although food and wine at meals were free. My customary pre-holiday sun lamp treatment to condition my skin to UV rays meant that I could soak up the sunshine.

In my chapter ('Sixties Cool') I talk about sharing a tanning cabin with the Geordie singer, Alan Price.

My French was pretty useless but it didn't matter; we drank, we swam, we frolicked and we had fun mixing and mingling at meals (table groups were allocated randomly) and we enjoyed chatting up girls at the bar.

There's a rugby club joke called 'the three-man lift'. Nat would claim he was the strongest man in the world and could lift up three people with one hand. The prank was one of the participants ended up with a glass of water poured down his pants. This was award-winning mature theatre at its best.

One of the GOs ('Gentils Organisateurs', a bit like redcoats at Butlins, but classier) called Michael Landwehr (something like that) enjoyed this and it was via him that Nat and I were invited to extend our holiday. No charge; we would just carry on being sociable with the Brits - and doing silly stuff on stage. The thought of doing this wasn't a problem for Nat who, with no disrespect to him, didn't have a full time job.

I was employed by IBM so 'Morre', one of the GOs typed an official looking letter explaining that I had suffered colitis and needed to defer my travel. He signed the letter with the name 'Dr Del Picure'. There should be an accent over the 'U' of the surname making it translatable to the English word 'injection'.

I wish I still had this letter, but I gave it to IBM to explain my unavoidable week of 'sick leave'.

A few months after our return, Nat joined Club Med as a G.O. so on my subsequent holiday at Club Med (at a different Greek location) I was welcomed as the 'le grand rouge' - referring more to my skin colour than that of my hair.

We became friendly with Perry Damone (son of Vic Damone) who seemed to be spending the summer at Club Med.

He was a nice lad (in his early twenties at the time) and I performed a few stage acts with him. Mainly comedy (at least that was the intention) and our ventriloquist and dummy routine appeared on a second evening due to popular demand. I wondered if we could support Vic Damone when he came to sing in UK but Perry seemed reluctant to mention it.

He was enrolled at an American College in Richmond so I met him a few times later in London. He's no longer with us, sadly, having died in his early fifties.

On this holiday, the 'chef du village', Bernard Pollack asked me to join the team to travel with them to Guadeloupe. I said I would 'think about it' but I suspect we both knew it wasn't something I could dare to do. The dilemma between 'serious me' with a 'proper job' (and not let down those who had made sacrifices for me) and that of becoming some irresponsible hedonist fun-seeker had only one outcome.

Slam went that sliding door I'm not surprised to say. Still, it was an option.

I enjoyed one more Club Med holiday (once again in Greece, or possibly Tunisia). This was a sporting-oriented base with a variety of French international athletes - fencing, weight lifting, judo and gymnastics. There were also a couple of rugby B team international players so we had two successful games of 'Guests vs. GO' rugby. My dynamic five yard try scoring run was the clincher in the second match.

For reasons I can't recall, I sang 'the leaving of Liverpool' as a stage duet with one of the camp staff. She later told me that she was a lesbian which might have been the truth – or perhaps a storyline to deter my advances. Even so, I was puzzled how she could resist a rugby international try scorer?

One of the visiting sportsmen was Jean-Paul Coche, a French Judo International; a lovely man who played second row with me in our rugby matches. He had never played the game beforehand and said he would rely on me to tell him what to do. His wife also pleaded with me to 'look after him'.

109

I never reached a top level in my sporting career but I'm proud to say that I scored one International Rugby try and that I coached the 1972 Munich Olympic Judo bronze medal winner.

CHAPTER 27

FRIVOLITY TO FRIVOLITY VIA A PROPER JOB

It was the random 'sliding doors' factor that got me employed at IBM. I really wanted to stay on at University; one more year of frivolous amateur dramatics and girl chasing seemed to fit my qualifications, but that option was denied to me. I drifted into interviews with the employment people who came to talk to us.

I had interviews with BBC, and even a 'voice test'. Imagine "Mr Gromyko, the Russian Foreign Secretary" booming out in a Berwick accent and it might explain why I didn't get offered a job; I eventually ended up being offered a job as a systems engineer at IBM.

I floundered on the first four-week course ('basic school') due to feeling overawed by all these serious business people. I joined earlier than I should have done and found myself amongst experienced business folk changing career. My test results on the course were pretty dire and I later discovered (by sneaking a look at my personnel file) that I came close to being 'let go'. I was living in a bedsitter just off Baker Street and feeling a bit lost. My University chums were all living with their parents.

I pleaded a case of disruption to my mental state and my manager gave me the benefit of the doubt and transferred me to a later group for my second course. Wow; there's a sliding door for you!

My training colleagues were now mainly new graduates and I enjoyed their company much more.

We studied the 421-accounting machine, a large electronic box about the size of a sideboard that read input data from holes punched in 80 column cards. We plugged wire leads into a

111

removable panel board to programme the machine so it produced invoices in the required format. This was pure mental logic and I was in my element. I did very well in the '421 programming' exam thanks to another 'sliding door'. This time it was a real door to a classroom cupboard that had been left open revealing a copy of the exam paper. I blame (or maybe thank) a colleague who discovered it. Purist could say we cheated but this paper had questions only, no answers giving us assistance that focussed our learning. That's my story and I'm sticking to it. I hope you do the same too, Peter Fairbairn, wherever you are.

Flush with my new success, my first job after this part of training was to work at 'Sun Engraving Ltd' (engraved photo plates for printing) in Holborn and programme (wire up) their new 421 accounting machine to produce their invoices. They were a small company (they engraved photo-plates for printing).

I worked with a lovely blonde lady called Veronica (who, a few years later, left her fiancé to set up home with a married IBM colleague) - but that's another story, and quite a shocking one in its day.

We worked at a spare desk in Brigadier Bright's office. He was the Managing Director. Our working day was like being part of a Gilbert and Sullivan musical but without the music. The Brigadier would enter mid-morning with a cheery wave and make a few phone calls (to characters with names like 'Pinky', 'Pongo' or 'Squiffy') to arrange lunch at his club. We would see him again briefly mid-afternoon when he came back and with a cheerier wave, collected his briefcase and set off home.

Our panel wiring was a great success and the Brigadier gave us each a glass of champagne when we'd finished. For a moment I wondered if his waving champagne bottle meant that he was going to launch the accounting machine as if it were a ship. It looked the part, being large and battleship grey in colour. The entire staff celebrated this momentous moment. I enjoyed the fuss and that day was one of the highlights of my IBM career.

My next four-week course was about the range of IBM computers – these were miniscule devices compared to today. Not in size (the opposite was true), but in terms of power. My first computer client work was on an IBM system that boasted 8K of memory. In physical size, it was like a row of tall cabinets standing on a raised floor in an air-conditioned room about the size of a school hall. To put things in perspective, the NASA moon landing in 1969 was controlled by an IBM computer with 64K memory.

In the mid nineteen seventies, I recall a half-meg memory (512K) upgrade being delivered to a client and needing a fork lift truck to lift it and a window removed to get it in the room. The resultant one and half megabytes of memory put this computer in the top ten largest systems in the UK. There's a lot more storage on the modern wristwatch and my banking app does more than these big processors used to do.

In the late nineteen sixties (1969) I did an assignment running courses for customers and IBM trainees; I was in my element; performing and showing off. This was a twelve-month assignment and I considered transferring full time to training but IBM's ethos seemed to compel people to 'move on and move up' and make it seem like a lack of ambition if you weren't always trying. I was urged to join the sales force. I can understand that as I was pretty personable, even if I say so myself (I just did) and on the eventual 'sales school' (a 'pass' or 'fail' course), I was second top of the class.

My problem with selling has always been my attitude. I didn't like the idea of 'hard selling' when someone seemed reluctant to buy. I could do it on a training course (evidently) but not in real life; I found it difficult to be enthusiastic about things I wasn't passionate about. Why wasn't I passionate about selling? That's too deep a question for me.

On and off I worked in the City of London. I started there in 1965 in the newly finished Moorgate and London Wall area and spent a few years there as a salesman in Finance Branch of IBM and later Banking Branch selling to Nat West Bank. Before the advertising and logo men came on to the scene, the bank was called 'National Westminster'. I used to make the (now non pc) joke that 'Nat West' sounded like a Jewish tailor. On a trip with the bank's IT executives to IBM development labs in California. I can remember one larger than life US visitor host asking us,

"So, which one of you four guys is Nat West?"

Every salesman (oops - salesperson) had the aim of achieving sales targets and joining that year's 'Hundred percent club'. Partly driven by money but, equally importantly, to get invited to that year's 'convention' held in exotic places like Monte Carlo, Vienna or Madrid. These were 'jollies' of the highest calibre with great entertainment. There'd be a compere like John Cleese, Michael Parkinson or Ronnie Corbett and top flight musicians and entertainers. I remember seeing Ella Fitzgerald, Ronnie Dankworth, Cleo Lane and Jazz bandleader Benny Green. I 'performed' in stage events with Ruth Madoc and (now Sir) John Tusa.

Rumour has it that I performed a strip tease in a Berlin nightclub in exchange for six bottles of champagne. Rumour also has it that I gave my name as 'Peter Morgan', the then UK Sales Director. As a 'temporary' performer, I was allowed to go backstage to 'come down' after my impressive act and I enjoyed mingling with the scantily clad dancing girls – so rumour has it also.

I think I was better known within IBM for my formal and informal stage performances at product launches and conventions than for any record-breaking sales achievements. In fact, I'm sure of it. Don't get me wrong, I did OK and IBM was good to me; I was paid well and I made good friends but I didn't conform as well as I could have done or should have done.

I had a series of management roles and I was reasonably good at them; mainly because my employees did the real work whilst I just cranked the 'keep them motivated' handle.

My final two years at IBM were as manager of sales and technical training before I resigned in January 1990, to become the third partner of CA (Cambridge Associates), a management consultancy group run by John Banks, an ex-IBM colleague. John had been my boss at one time in IBM when I worked in banking sector, (my boss's boss, in fact). CA had taken on big sales training contracts with Rank Xerox and BT, so my pedigree and reputation was worth something.

My leaving IBM puzzled my dad. With his life's experiences he couldn't understand why I would leave a secure job and was worried that I had been sacked.

I confess that I, too, wrestled with the concept of leaving IBM; in those days it was a secure 'cradle-to-grave' organisation that worked hard at dissuading good people from leaving. I'm not bigging myself up by using the phrase 'good people' as I knew that my exit was classified in the 'very much regret' category; the highest level of regret thereby putting my final act in IBM at the highest category of classification.

Leave them on a high, that's what I say!

Susie, of course, having worked in theatre kept reminding me that it was just a job ('for Goodness sake!') and that life would go on – as, indeed it did and got better. She pushed me through that 'sliding door', bless her x.

I eventually became the sole-proprietor and owner of the new one man band known as Cambridge Associates. As the years passed, my roleplay acting and toastmaster work increased and, in 2008, I wound-up CA.

I have now evolved into the playacting and performing kind of person that Susie always swore she would avoid having as a husband.

She's still with me though, I'm delighted to say.

CHAPTER 28

A TALE OF TWO WINE BARS (AND TWO MARRIAGES)

◆━━━━━━━━━━●━━━━━━━━━●◆

This chapter heading is a play on words of 'A Tale of Two Cities' by Charles Dickens which tells the tale of a sacrifice made for the greater good. The hero, Sydney Carton sacrifices himself (on the guillotine) so that Charles Darnay can escape the clutches of the French Revolution mob and marry Lucie, a lady beloved by both men.

I'm not claiming such a parallel in my circumstances but on the 'sliding-doors' principle that I've mentioned previously, my 'sacrifice' of enduring a bad first marriage meant that I was in the position to enjoy a good second one. No physical sacrifice was required although it came a bit close during my first marriage but I'll spare everyone the details.

Oddly enough, wine bars had a role in both of my wedding situations. Two in particular; 'The Loose Box' in High Street Kensington' and 'Finos Wine Bar' in Mayfair. Both of these, I'm pretty certain they will have metamorphosed into different establishments. I haven't been back to check for 'blue plaques' noting my visits.

In the nineteen seventies (and probably still today), wine bars were popular venues to mix and mingle with members of the opposite sex (or of the same sex if that floats your boat) in order to flirt and 'pull' (as the saying goes). These wine bars were very popular gathering places at the end of a working day and some people would go straight from the office whilst others went home to change first. Ladies had the choice of being 'chatted up' by rather sweaty men looking dishevelled in crumpled business suits (who were pretty drunk by 8pm), or by smoother and sweeter smelling chaps wearing their best casual attire.

I, and my single men friends (and the occasional married man) would visit the 'Loose Box' on Thursday (after rugby training) and occasionally on a Friday. Gradually the Thursday outings replaced formal rugby training. Susie (my wife!) claims that Friday attendees are less choosy and more desperate as the 'must-get-fixed-up-for-weekend' deadline is imminent.

I met her on a Friday.

The wine bar socialising 'model' works well. None of us were wine buffs but clutching a bottle of, usually cheap, white wine in a crowded gathering made it easy to mix and mingle and get chatting with winning sentences like, "Can I offer you a drink of my very expensive wine?" Our 'social distancing' targets were set at no more than eighteen inches. Suggestive looks, blatant flirting and friendly touching didn't result in law suits or 'me too' protests. The rules were the same for women too; so we obviously took equality seriously.

There was a late-night bar (Mr Pips) near the Hilton Hotel in Mayfair that had a late licence as long as the patrons bought a food ticket. The entrance fee got you a ticket for some bread and cheese as well as being redeemable for your first drink. I'm not saying we went there a lot, but the bouncer on the door that controlled entry gave us VIP status so we could jump the queue. However, that's introducing a third bar so I'm not extending my tale to include it as I didn't marry any of the ladies I met there.

It was a Friday in March 1981 when my IBM mate David Godfrey and I went to Finos. On Susie's classification, we were the second shift of men who had been home to change. The bar was narrow and crowded and Susie was of the view that if she, as a pretty lady, got to the end of the bar without being offered a drink, the evening was a failure. She was with her small friend Cathy and I was with my small friend David. Susie and Cathy had started at this bar several hours previously (with the 'first shift'), they then went to The Loose Box and, having failed there decided to give Finos a final despairing try.

I remember this lovely Charlotte Rampling lookalike (close) in a red jumpsuit suddenly appearing in front of me, a dishevelled and vaguely Sean Connery lookalike. Susie told me later that my big chest and green pullover with the words 'Cyprus Rugby Tour 1980' emblazoned on it made a barrier impossible to pass. She read aloud the words on my sweater (as you do) and decided to cut her losses and stay with us. The fact that David popped up from the bar with a fresh bottle and four glasses was the clincher.

We stayed at Finos to finish the bottle and probably another before piling into my car to drive to a Bistro in High Street Kensington for dinner – with wine, naturally. David and Cathy sat in the back seat; Cathy was rather a buxom girl, which didn't go unnoticed by David. "Very handy these men from the north", she told Susie later.

I then drove everyone back to Mayfair so Susie could collect her car and, having swopped phone numbers and snogged a little we drove our separate ways.

A few days later, David asked me if I was planning to 'see that girl again'. I did indeed see 'that girl' again and the rest, as they say, is history.

Just to add a wine postscript: Our wedding reception (5th November 1982) was at Chelsea Football Club Trophy room (organised by my rugby friend, Graham Franklin). That aspect of the business was under receivership and we enjoyed good quality champagne at a very low price. The exact opposite to how life was in our fateful wine bars.

CHAPTER 29

MY MUSICAL LIFE

My first extended play record (EP) for my red Dansette record player was 'Barber's Best' featuring Chris Barber and his Band. I bought it via 'Exchange and Mart', the go-to buy/sell magazine of the day. I paid one shilling and three pence (about six pence in today's money) and that included postage.

I became a trad jazz fan and bought a clarinet for £10 at a Market Stall in Newcastle. My schoolfriend David Rhind had a trumpet and we had great plans to form a band. Trouble was, we never had music lessons and relied on 'A Tune A Day' books, so our progress was limited.

David and I would go to see Jazz bands playing at Newcastle; Chris Barber, Gerry Brown, Kenny Ball, Acker Bilk but the highlight trip was when we went to see Louis Armstrong.

It was May 1962 and The Louis Armstrong All Stars were on their third British tour. I was an eighteen-year old jazz fan and travelling to Newcastle to see 'Satchmo' live was a dream come true. The nickname, we read, came from Louis' habit of using his mouth like a satchel to hold coins ('satchel mouth'). As a kid, he danced for pennies in the streets of New Orleans and he would scoop the coins into his mouth to stop bigger children stealing them.

On stage, the great man lived up to the image we had of him; incredible trumpet playing, bulging eyes, his famous gravel voice and hearty laugh – and a large pile of white linen handkerchiefs on the piano top for him to wipe his face.

After the show my friend and I went to the stage door, hoping to get an autograph. We expected to hand in our programmes and get them returned signed. We didn't anticipate a face-to-face meeting. Trummy Young, the All-Stars trombone player (another legend!) came to get us. He told us that Louis was tired but would be delighted to meet us, and he requested, very courteously, if we would keep our visit brief.

Our hero was sitting in a comfortable armchair. He was wearing jazzy striped pyjamas and a dressing gown. His jet-black silk suit was hanging behind him with his white (perspiration sodden) shirt lying crumpled on the floor.

What do you say when you meet a boyhood hero? In this case, it didn't matter. When he saw us, his face split into a huge grin, displaying gleaming white teeth and some dazzling gold fillings. We shook hands and he introduced us to his band members, one by one. Trummy Young, Billy Kyle, Barney Bigard, Mort Herbert, Danny Barcelona, Velma Middeleton – each one a legend. He made us feel like important dignitaries and not star-struck schoolboy jazz fans.

On my programme I had listed the tunes he had played and he compared my list with his original running order and said a few words about how he decided what to play. Louis asked me to select a page of the programme which he then signed in bright green ink and he did the same for my friend.

We told him we had enjoyed the concert; a comment he must have heard hundreds of times. His face split into another huge grin, as if he was receiving this compliment for the first time. 'My pleasure, my pleasure,' he said, 'glad you enjoyed it'.

For some reason, I told him I was learning to play the clarinet and my friend was learning to play trumpet. 'Hey, that's great', he said, 'Did you hear that?' he called out to the band members. Suddenly we were all jazz playing kindred spirits and his huge hand shook mine again.

After a while, Louis started to look tired so, remembering our promise to Trummy Young, we thought it was time to leave. 'A real pleasure to meet you', Louis said, and shook our hands once more.

'Hey kids', he called out as we were leaving, 'Keep blowin' and you'll make good music'. And he laughed again.

An unforgettable experience and I still have my programme signed in green ink.

There's a long gap in my music playing life after that. I tootled on my clarinet but never got beyond 'a tune a day book one'. I blame Dad in part. He would joke and comment to visitors, "Billy is learning the clarinet and I want him to play 'Over the hills and far away'" and everyone would laugh. He meant no harm, of course, but it scarred a sensitive boy like me. It made me understand that I should never discourage or disparage my children's efforts at anything they tried to do.

The music playing bug was always there though and I was about fifty-five when I enrolled on a saxophone playing class in Twickenham. The tutor was Tony Woods, and he did a great job in harnessing the class enthusiasm and inspiring us to play.

That class led to me and two band friends (Angie King and John Dilworth) starting 'St Margaret's Elastic Band'. We found a willing bandmaster in David Kaile, a local teacher who wanted to start a band and after a few pub meetings with a handful of other players, we started to meet every week. David provided the music and I became the de-facto organiser. My efficiency, sense of precision and eye for detail obviously shone through! I can claim credit (and these are my memoirs after all) for organising the email list, collecting subscriptions, setting up our website and Facebook group. I was subtly creating a dependency on me that would overlook any music playing limitations.

The band has evolved and changed over the years but getting involved with it is one of the best things I've done. It's fun, it's stimulating and I've made some good friends. Playing music is a great leveller; you leave your day-to-day identity behind. We have / have had an eclectic mix of people in the band: CEO, Doctor, Chess-Master, Roofer, Professor; Soldier, Adult Swimming Teacher, Actor, Instrument Maker; Schoolteacher, Pilot and me. We've even got the mum of Chis Martin (Coldplay).

We play regular local 'gigs'; mainly at outdoor Summer and Christmas events. We are the regular band supporting Remembrance Sunday at Richmond and we have produced various 'lockdown virtual performances' during the 2020 Covid-19 pandemic. All visible on the band website at elasticband.org.

A few years ago, Lucy started playing harmonica and I have now followed suit. It's a lovely portable instrument and has come into its own as I get ga-ga and as my teeth start to fail. It's a fun instrument and I'm keen to learn. I'm determined not to repeat my clarinet false start and I'm doing internet-based lessons.

I've told my tennis playing friend Dave Kelly that I'm planning to replace Paul Jones in his 'Blues Band'.

I bet PJ is worried.

CHAPTER 30

'BETTER THAN ANYTHING YOU SEE IN THE WEST END

◆•————————•—————————•◆

Looking back on my life, I find it intriguing how an intensely shy person, such as I am, could develop into a reasonably successful speaker and performer. The secret, if there is one, goes beyond 'faking it until you make it'; it's more 'faking it until you become it'.

Acting is a form of 'faking it' and becoming the person that the director demands you to be. I spent many hours doing that at school and at university which undoubtedly impeded my academic progression but which, I have no doubt, enhanced me as a person. Amateur dramatics has been my great confidence builder.

School plays started me off. My role as an eleven-year old nativity shepherd, where I would say, "this must be Bethlehem we are nearing" oozed so much confidence (and volume) that the director, Mr Whitehouse, asked me to tone it down. The role became something I could hide behind and keep the 'inner me' protected – albeit only for three performances.

A main characteristic of 'AmDram' performances is that they tend to play to full houses and audiences are effusive in their praise.

'Better than anything you could see in the West End', and other phrases of that ilk are quite common and, of course, completely unjustified. Family members and friends see these performances through rose tinted spectacles and, in offering words of encouragement, often lose a sense of true perspective!

My amateur dramatic years in London were major influences on my life socially and in terms of opportunities to perform and show off - and as a source of girlfriends. Everything about our amateur dramatic group was great fun; the rehearsals, the camaraderie, the performances and the after-show parties. Even building the set was an enjoyable social event.

After my 1972 performance as 'Barnet' in The National Health, a Peter Nicholls black comedy performed at the old Vic in 1969, several people said that I was 'better than Jim Dale'. He, Jim, played my part in the original production or, to be more accurate, I played the part he established on stage and screen in the 'Stanhope Theatre Production' (my amateur group) a few years later in London.

My performance was good (even though I say so myself) but, I will reluctantly concede, possibly not quite as good as that of Jim Dale. Possibly not.

During my years with the drama group, I made some good friends who became famous professionally; Carol Royle and the dear departed Alan Rickman to name only two.

Both of these people were active participants in our group, and staunch supporters beyond their formal drama school training and graduation. I keep in touch with Carol and see her from time although, nowadays our lives move in very different orbits.

Alan was one of the first people I met when I joined 'Court Drama Group' in 1969. My rugby playing friend, Bill Rodwell told me about the group during a spring rugby tour to Ireland and I'm forever grateful that he took me along shortly afterwards. The group was run by Miriam and Wilfrid Sharpe (teachers at Latymer School in West London) and Alan Rickman had been one of their pupils. At the time I met him, he was working as a graphic artist and designer and, of course, very keen on drama. Even at a young age, his talent shone.

Alan was destined for greater theatrical things and, after a surprising amount of soul searching (in the pub), he applied for, and won a scholarship to RADA. He never forgot his roots though and kept in touch throughout his career – and indeed throughout his life. Cancer took him from us and he died in January 2016.

In 1972 I played opposite his girlfriend / partner and eventual wife, Rima Horton in Neil Simon's play, 'Come Blow Your Horn'. I was the male lead (called Alan, coincidentally), Rima played my girlfriend and Alan Rickman showed his artistic skill in designing the set!

Rima's brother, Tim, played my younger brother and, at a crucial moment during the play, he had the line 'Holy mackerel, I've got two fathers!'. At one performance, Tim cried out, 'Holy father, I've got two mackerels!'. He would have got away with his error had he not muttered an expletive before correcting himself. On the rare occasions that the drama group members get together (sadly, mainly at funerals nowadays), we remind Tim about this.

Our group secretary wrote to the play's author, Neil Simon, telling him about this incident and he sent a charming reply, typed using an old-fashioned typewriter, stating, 'I think your student has possibly improved my play'.

Modesty prevents me listing my fifteen or so performances but I have many happy memories and a few highlights. One was when I was asked, at short notice, to play 'Nick' in Edward's Albee's 'Who's Afraid of Virginia Woolf' as the original actor fell ill. I had three weeks to learn the script and to rehearse. Not unduly difficult for a full-time actor but I had to spend my daytime doing my 'proper job' – and get a haircut. My rather dishevelled scruffy look (which was fashionable at the time) didn't suit Nick's clean-cut all-American boy image. My employers at IBM were pleasantly surprised at my conversion to the required corporate image. This was probably the second-best thing I've done (my performance, I mean, not my clean-up – although that was pretty good too).

In 1971, played Alan Rickman's father in 'Backbone', a play by Michael Rosen and we shared one memorable scene where we were forced to improvise through thirty seconds of unexpected power blackout. It was at a point in the play where I was telling a corny joke and Alan, as my son, was supposed to give visual reactions which, in the darkness, he replaced with appropriate audible grunts and sighs. The scene worked very well, thanks to Alan's supportive improvisation but we decided not to repeat it at our subsequent performances.

Darkness featured again during our 1973 Christmas show. Ted Heath, the UK Prime Minister, introduced measures to save fuel during a miner's dispute and electricity supplies were constrained. Our show went on with 'Victorian' feel to it. We had battery powered lamps and lanterns some of which we would pass between us as part of the action. Only a small band of privileged actors can say that, as they made an entrance, Alan Rickman handed them a lamp.

The highlight of my amateur acting career was playing 'Malcolm' in David Halliwell's 1965 play, 'Little Malcolm and His Struggle Against the Eunuchs'. The original play (and subsequent film) starred John Hurt, David Warner and Rosalind Ayres. We got a very favourable review by Isha Mellor in the March 1973 edition of 'Plays and Players', a theatregoer's magazine. She was kind enough to write a lengthy letter saying that her review text 'was very much cut' and including her original text in full. She said nice things about all of us and I still treasure her letter.

'Scrawdyke, the outlawed art student (me) swung with style a voluminous coat with cropped sleeves. He was ruthless in his command of his supporters, yet full of fun'

Court Drama Group, later called Stanhope Theatre Company, was a source of fun and joy for me from 1969 to 1976. It started as part of the London Borough 'Enrich Your Leisure' scheme. In those days, people were encouraged to enrol on evening classes for enjoyment and 'enrichment' - and not purely as part of career development. Most of the classes were free of charge. An eclectic bunch of people joined our group, or were already there before I joined. Noel Howard (another person, sadly no longer with us) was very senior in Monty Burman theatrical costumier, so we got great outfits. In one comedy sketch Alan Rickman wore Ron Moody's Fagin costume and I wore a kilt that Richard Harris was scheduled to use. We knew this because the labels were still attached.

Alan's mischievous nature came to the fore when he encouraged me to cross out the words 'Richard Harris' and insert 'William Freeman' in their place. Richard presumably got his costume when he needed it as I wasn't called on to play the role. Alan left his 'Ron Moody' label intact – probably very wise, considering his chosen career.

Like most amateur groups, we played to reasonably full houses, mainly because we made great efforts to sell tickets to friends and family. There's an unwritten theatrical rule that, when the number of cast members exceed that of the audience, the show can be cancelled and money refunded.

The only experience I have of this was during a revue we ran at YMCA Theatre Bristol over the University Easter holiday period in 1965.

The show was called 'Who Cares?' and was a mixture of comedy and musical sketches. It had been a great success at University, so we decided to try a short professional run. One or two of our cast members went on to greater things, although not directly as a result of this show. Sue Lawley became a broadcaster, Chris de Souza a BBC music guru and composer and Bruce Millar a musical star and radio producer in South Africa.

These 'professional' performances were during my final year at University and I wouldn't have missed them for anything but, logically, it was crazy for me to be spending time performing instead of studying for my exams.

Of our ten performances during our 'run', we cancelled three times due to lack of audience numbers. Other evenings, we roped in friends and front-of-house staff to fill seats and we would slip from backstage whenever we could to swell numbers so our(few) paying audience individuals wouldn't feel awkward.

'Who Cares?' was a very well written show and it was a shame that many people missed it. Maybe they were the people who didn't care?

That was their loss.

After all, like every performance I was involved in, it was 'better than anything they could have seen in the West End'

CHAPTER 31

'I ONCE MET...'

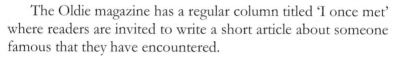

The Oldie magazine has a regular column titled 'I once met' where readers are invited to write a short article about someone famous that they have encountered.

I've made a few submissions, none of which have been published (yet). Here they are:

I ONCE MET THE QUEEN MOTHER

Of the many thousands of people who have met Queen Elizabeth, the late Queen Mother, my encounter was the result of a misunderstanding by Her Majesty.

It was the summer of 1984, and I had been invited to a 'business event' at Epsom racecourse where I could enjoy free hospitality and watch horse racing. As a salesman and later, a manager in IBM I had been to these kinds of event many times. We had hosted quite a few of them but this time, I was on the receiving end.

As part of the deal I, with every one of the other guests, was expected to listen to our hosts telling us all the amazing ways they could help our businesses grow. In those days, I suffered from a low threshold of boredom (which still exists today) and exhortations along the lines of 'your company data is a key asset and we can help you exploit it' tended to send me into a coma. It's not that I didn't care (I didn't care much; I have to say) but I had heard it all before. It's the sort of guff I had presented myself at similar events; I've even written books about it. My son, Tom, would refer to the 'six steps of the sale'. This was a line from a movie that a boring Dad would quote and, to my horror, Tom regarded me in a similar light. Not always, I'm glad to say.

To avoid a 'six steps of the sale' style presentation, at the first opportunity, I excused myself to go and watch the horseracing. To go anywhere really.

Wandering aimlessly, I went down a set of stairs, nodded confidently at a uniformed commissionaire in my best 'of-course-I'm-allowed-here' manner and found myself in a smart enclosure area where a military brass band was in full flow.

I love brass band music and went closer to the bandstand so I could hear it better. I thought it extremely courteous when the conductor suddenly turned towards me and saluted with a flourish. I bowed my head and nodded in response to this kind gesture and then I noticed an elegant and petite old lady standing a few yards to my left, who gave a refined wave to acknowledge the band conductor's salute.

The Queen Mother (for it was her) then turned to look at me. She smiled graciously and said, 'is everything alright?'. 'Yes, Ma'am,' I bowed my head in response and then stood smartly to attention to look like the protection officer she had obviously mistaken me for. 'Everything is fine, Your Majesty.'

'Very good,' she said, 'please carry on' and she turned to the conductor and signalled for him to continue the music.

I reversed slowly towards the stairs where a gathering of tall men in dark suits and wearing earpieces, were looking at me with puzzled expressions.

I said to them in my most authoritative voice, 'Her Majesty has told me to carry on'.

And I ran back up the stairs

I ONCE MET ALBERT FINNEY

In 1963, I had a six-week summer job at Butlins Holiday camp in Minehead, Somerset. I wanted to raise some pocket money and have a bit of a fling before I started my second year at Bristol University. I had spent the previous summer at the Filey camp and enjoyed it so much that I wanted to repeat the experience. The pay was fairly modest but there was fun to be had.

One evening, my workmates and I had gathered, as usual, in the central dance hall and bar area to have a few drinks and a few laughs - and also to flirt with the waitresses. It was generally forbidden or, at least, frowned on, for staff members to engage with guests in any kind of amorous way. This was a fairly academic rule as far as a shy boy like me was concerned; besides, chatting to our waitress colleagues was challenge enough.

I was aware of Albert Finney from his earlier movie, 'Saturday Night and Sunday Morning' and I was convinced that he was sitting, with a male friend, in the seats alongside the dance area. You don't expect a film star to be visiting a Butlins Holiday Camp and we had quite a bit of 'is it?', 'isn't it?' debate. (In hindsight it made sense for it to be him as his film 'Tom Jones' was being shot in the area).

I wanted to confirm my suspicion so I started to manoeuvre to get a closer look whilst trying to look nonchalant. My stalking skills weren't up to scratch or maybe my lingering stale kitchen-worker scent preceded my approach. Whatever the reason, Albert suddenly turned his head and looked at me. My natural eloquence and fluency momentarily deserted me; I hadn't planned to speak but I blurted, "You're Albert Finney".

A flicker of a smile came on his face, "Yes' he said, 'I know".

There was an awkward silence for a moment so, as a finish to our 'lifelong buddies meet up chat', I thrust out my hand which he shook briefly, then turned away to talk to his friend.

I've been waiting all my life for someone to ask the question, 'did you ever meet Albert Finney?'.

'Yes', I would reply, 'we had a long chat one summer at Butlins holiday camp'.

I ONCE MET THE RED ARROWS

It was the spring of 1981 and my friend David Godfrey and I were on holiday in Fowey, Cornwall. I'd been there before on a rugby weekend and stayed at the 'King of Prussia' (KOP) hotel on the harbour front. A friendly and cozy establishment, enhanced by the mad nature of David Mackenzie, the landlord.

This was U.K.O.B.A. week (United Kingdom Offshore Boating Association) so the place was a frenzy of boating and sailing activities accompanied by lots of singing and drinking in the pub. In all of the pubs, actually.

The 'Red Arrows' were the highlight of the week. We were gathered in the harbour square, looking out to sea with the steep hill of Fowey behind us. A background noise built up and the iconic planes roared overhead in formation, spewing their red, white and blue colours. They performed their impressive criss-crossing manoeuvres accompanied by our yelling, waving and screaming. They didn't hear us, of course; it made no sense for us to shout. A pilot wasn't going to tell his flight leader to be quiet so he could listen to our cheering.

The pilots were the centre of attention in the KOP pub that evening. Six pilots and a couple of senior squadron leader types all looking like 'Biggles', the pilot hero from the W.E.Johns action books that men of my generation will remember. As boys we enjoyed referring to 'The White Fokker', the first in the series of such books. I think the politically correct establishment eventually had it removed from Amazon.

David and I enjoyed talking to these young men, trying to bask in their glory and to curry favour with the girls that flocked to them. They were career RAF pilots and this was a short-term assignment for them; the Red Arrows ensemble would change every few months.

Even so, I thought, what a great time they would have living this 'Biggles' style glamorous life; flying planes, impressing crowds, being the centre of attention, 'pulling' girls. I must have voiced these thoughts because the squadron leader chap, smiled at me and said, "I can tell you that you are exactly the kind of person we are NOT looking for".

CHAPTER 32

HOSPITALS

◆———————————•———————————•◆

I've been lucky compared to my parents and others of their generation. Mam, despite her strength and resilience, spent time in hospital as result of her heart problems and had valve replacement surgery in 1971. I've written about Dad's problems and he drew a very short straw regarding health. Coal mining didn't help and the rigours of war years meant that he was technically ill all of his life, frail and needing regular medical intervention. Much of this was routine for him – apart from a ruptured appendix which took him from Berrington to Edinburgh hospital for emergency surgery.

When I was in my early forties, I had a luxurious stay at a private clinic in Wimbledon for a hernia operation. I had full medical insurance cover in those days, so I jumped at the chance of choosing the date for my operation and of having a private recovery room.

My children, Lucy and Tom were three and four years old respectively and I can recall their worried faces (bless them) when Susie brought them in to see me after my surgery. The care was so good that when I was given the option of staying an extra night, I opted to do so. My only moment of concern was just before my anaesthetic when the staff started talking about the FA Cup Final due to be played the next day and as I slipped into unconsciousness, I was willing them to forget the match and to concentrate on the most important piece of surgery of their careers!

I've had my share of Accident & Emergency trips as a result of rugby injuries; broken collar bone, broken ankle, stitching to my eyebrows and a couple of more serious non-private hospital stays over my seven decades.

The big one (my 2016 heart surgery) follows this Chapter. My earlier (circa 1948) experience was to do with an easier medical condition but it took place during the days when hospitals were more rigorous and stricter than they are today.

I had, I think, some kind of gastric problem that blocked my intestines. Basically, I couldn't 'poo'. I can remember having a swollen tummy and I kept wobbling over, finding it difficult to stand. The cure, I think, was a regular series of enemas (I'm glad my memory is a bit vague!). I was taken to hospital and stayed there for three weeks. Visiting hours were very strict and my parents were only allowed to visit me once a week

The Mam and Dad visit was the highlight of my stay; I had a cot bed with large sides to stop me falling out (or running away!) and lay proudly in the middle of the male ward waiting to see them.

Screens appeared around me from time to time as an army of white-coated medics with plastic tubes, funnels, hot water and buckets did unmentionable things that forced the shit out of me. They were probably normal procedures but my mind seems to have blanked them.

Every day, Albert Inglis (who, in later years, would work with my Dad at Blackburn and Price Garage in Berwick) came over and read me a story. I would anticipate this and get very excited as I saw him walk over to me. He featured again in my life many years later when he taught me to swim. I am not a great swimmer, but I got the anti-drowning basics from Albert. These swimming lessons were in the North Sea at Berwick in pools that filled with the tide; luxuries like custom built indoor pools hadn't yet been invented – so I have some excuse for my aquatic ineptitude.

Dad spent many days of his life in hospital after the end of the Second World War as a result of his tuberculosis and, in later years, for breathing and nervous disorders. His final days in March 1987 were spent in Berwick Infirmary where he had been sent to give Mam a break from looking after him. He was dealt an unfair hand in the lottery of life but he bore it well and lived every breath to do the best he could for his family. As did Mam. Bless them both xx.

Mam had heart valve replacement surgery in 1971 at Shotley Bridge hospital near Morpeth, Northumberland. This was pretty serious stuff and she was told it had a seventy percent chance of success and, all being well, could add an extra seven years to her life (she was a tough cookie and lived a further twenty-seven years). Dad and I stayed overnight before and after her surgery. The hospital had a small apartment with recliner chairs; we didn't sleep well the night before Mam's operation but had moments of unscheduled light relief when one of our recliner chairs would 'over-recline' and tip us on the floor.

Decades later when I had heart surgery (more on that later) the recovery process had me up and walking the next day; visitors were allowed anytime and I was sent home after four days. It wasn't like that with Mam; she was kept in bed for several days and visitors had to wear gowns, surgical boots and a face mask. All for very good reasons at the time. The team did great work with Mam and I sent a large bouquet of flowers to Sister Ritson (her name is forever lodged in my brain). The flowers will have died long ago but I hope Sister R and her staff are still fit and well.

Lucy has avoided hospital; I'm delighted to say and I hope that continues – apart from baby producing time – and Tom has had a couple of stays; firstly, at Kings Lynn hospital when he suffered a whooping breathing difficulty that alarmed the visiting GP when we stayed with Susie's parents. Another time Tom got pneumonia aged about five, and I did the overnight shift staying with him while Susie did the day shift. Tom got a little worried about his condition, bless him and my eyes still water at the memory of him asking, 'am I going to die?'.

A few years later, Tom had surgery to remove adenoids and my heart-stopping image was of the gowned surgeon walking towards us after the operation. It's a standard TV programme drama scene that usually heralds devastating news. Not this time, thankfully, we were just being told it had taken longer than expected to staunch the bleeding. He had two nights in intensive care just to verify that all was OK.

Lucy had a minor skirmish when we had to take her to Kings Lynn Fire Station so a fireman could use a clever cutting device to remove a ring she had stuck on her finger. We tease her about this every time we drive past the fire station.

In November 2019, Susie had surgery to resolve an ongoing back problem. Spacers were inserted in her spinal column to remove pressure from the sciatic nerve. We had met her surgeon (Kevin O'Neil) ten years previously and he deferred surgery at that time. This was a traumatic and expensive experience for Susie, but Kevin did a great job.

I don't enjoy staying in hospital (although I'm eternally grateful to the medical profession, both private and public, for everything they do) but I like it far less when my wife or children go there!

POSTSCRIPT – My Teeth

This topic isn't worth a separate chapter but I have quite a few 'medical related' memories (some painful!) about dentistry and my teeth.

As a young boy, I never looked after my teeth; I don't remember tooth cleaning rituals and my childhood took place before anyone thought of putting fluoride in the water.

No wonder I visited the dentist quite a lot.

Our Berwick based dentists were 'Tippet and Hare' - although 'Burke and Hare' would have been equally appropriate (these two characters committed sixteen murders in the early part of nineteenth century and sold the bodies for anatomy lecture dissection).

Norman Tippet and Bartram Hare drilled teeth with a chain driven drill and without giving any anaesthetic. My teeth were stuffed with mercury amalgam, the filling of the day and I had a lot of dentistry in later years to remove this poison. A tooth extraction (and I had a couple of these) was a major event, requiring Doctor Dewar (our GP) to administer chloroform via a face mask. A truly awful experience.

To be fair to Burke and Hare (sorry, Tippet and Hare), dentistry was primitive compared to today. Cosmetic dentistry hadn't been thought of and the purpose seemed purely to remove toothache. It was quite normal for middle aged people (in their forties) to have all their teeth pulled and to wear dentures.

By the time I got to my mid-twenties I had lost two top front teeth and two at the bottom – and I wore small dental plates. A lot of young Australian dentists came to London in the mid-sixties and brought a more up to date outlook on dentistry. I moved from NHS dentures to posher versions made of chrome and then to 'porcelain crowns and bridges' (a few of which I still have today). In later years as I grew more wealthy and increasingly vain, I had some dental implants to support the beaming smile I show today.

These are now beginning to wobble slightly and my very up market dentist in Kingston mutters about how they will need replacing in the 'foreseeable future'. Not if I can help it lady; I'm brushing, flossing and adding my Corsodyl paste probably more often than I need to.

I had intravenous sedation for my implant treatment. I was told that this would be like a normal anaesthetic but that I 'wouldn't be asleep' and I 'wouldn't remember anything'.

"Does that mean I could be screaming in agony but can't remember?"

An important question, I thought but I didn't get an answer from the dentist; he just laughed.

Anyway, that's enough about my dental worries; I'll put them out of my mind and keep smiling.

CHAPTER *33*

BECOMING A 'CABBAGE'

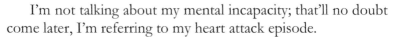

I'm not talking about my mental incapacity; that'll no doubt come later, I'm referring to my heart attack episode.

In the movies, we see grimacing, chest clutching, staggering and, more often than not, high drama, before our hero plummets to the ground with his scripted heart attack. Paddles appear from nowhere and with repeated shouts of 'clear!' the victim has his chest shocked with an electric charge – giving the opportunity for more physical acting.

It's not always like that in real life. Many of the twenty thousand yearly heart attacks in the UK start with an ache in the belly, rather like indigestion. That's what happened to me. I thought I had indigestion during my wedding toastmaster work on the Saturday (before Fathers' day 2106) but my pain was still there the following morning.

Susie, my life-saving rock, took me to casualty for a check-up. Lucy, our daughter, was asleep at our house; she had come to celebrate Fathers' day with Susie and I and brother Tom.

If your bellyache is diagnosed as a possible blood flow restriction, before you know it, you are whipped into a cardiac emergency unit, a miniscule camera is injected into an appropriate vein and screen images appear showing a snake like object wiggling inside your blood vessels.

'Where is it now?' I expected an answer along the lines of, 'near the top of your arm and about to turn right.' I didn't get this SatNav style response. 'We're moving around inside your heart, please lie still'. There was no need for the nurse to repeat her answer.

The 1966 movie 'Fantastic Voyage' came to mind. This film featured Raquel Welch (of all people) who, as part of a team of scientists inside a submarine, was miniaturised and injected into the vein of the movie hero. They then drove around in his bloodstream obliterating blockages to his blood flow.

Sixty years later, this movie scenario seems to have come true – apart from the miniaturised submarine and the Raquel Welch involvement. The 'injected camera' mechanism cleared my blockages temporarily and diagnosed the need for 'coronary artery bypass graft' surgery, thereby making me one of the twenty thousand people who would join the exclusive 'CABG' ('cabbage') club that year.

Susie and Lucy visited me when I was back up in a ward bed. She (Susie) had, quite rightly gone home to tell Lucy and Tom and to have some breakfast.

I was shocked by this situation but, surprisingly, not scared (too much). I was scheduled for surgery three days later but they deferred me due to an emergency. I hope my substitute survived his / her operation. I stayed in the ward for six more days. They wouldn't let me go home and I guess they used that time to get all my vital statistics OK. I had daily measurements, blood tests, a couple of X-rays while I hung around watching other patients come and go. Someone from my family visited me most days, which was wonderfully loving of them as it's not a particularly enjoyable experience and the journey is awful.

Oddly, or perhaps not, the hanging around calmed me. I saw people arrive, have their scheduled surgery and go home three days later. During my six-day wait, I moved bed three times, although I couldn't detect a logic.

'Another step nearer the operating theatre!' I thought, but then I'd move further away.

Susie came to see me the day before my surgery and offered to come the following day. I'm sure she was a bit worried and, bless her, I know she thought I was worried.

The medical 'procedure' (a less daunting word than 'surgery') is very efficient and surprisingly informal. You are part of a ward of twenty or so anxious souls waiting for, or recovering from cardiac surgery. When your moment is due, you walk (yes, walk) the short distance to the operating theatre.

When I did my short walk, escorted by my preparation nurse and ward sister, the other surgical inmates waved and wished me luck, reminding me of movie scenes where the 'death row victim' is escorted to his fate whilst the other inmates rattle their cell doors and yell abuse.

'Can I have your book if you don't come back?' I tried to offer a genuine smile to my enquiring bed neighbour but my mind was reviewing the 'ninety-eight per cent success' figure I had been quoted, I was also trying to assess the implications of being operation number six in the twenty scheduled for that week – and, more worryingly, number eight-four in the hundred that would be done that month.

I wasn't un-worried but I was quite calm. Tom and Lucy sent me lovely text messages which touched me. Bless them; I was determined for my family to avoid the shock and problem of me not surviving. I was muttering their names when my go-to-sleep-needle was put in my arm.

Six hours later you wake to the greeting 'you've had your procedure' (there's that word again) and discover they've harvested veins from your left leg, sawn open your rib cage, frozen you to sub-zero temperature, put you on a heart bypass machine, attached segments of your stolen veins to make new blood flow bypass routes - and then neatly stitched you up again.

I confess to one wobbly moment. 'Can I phone my wife?' I asked the recovery nurse, 'I'm not sure I'm going to survive all this'. 'Phone her now and you probably won't,' was the instant reply, 'it's one thirty in the morning'.

I didn't make the call.

Four days later you are declared fit to go home and sent on your way; a fully qualified member of the Cabbage Club - CABG 1, 2, 3, 4 or rarely 5 determined by your number of bypass grafts. I was a CABG 4 and rather proud of my senior positioning in the club pecking order.

No one would volunteer to join this exclusive club; it doesn't rank high on any 'bucket lists', but if membership is recommended, hand yourself over to our wonderful NHS surgical people and to our wonderful NHS care system – both of which are even more wonderful than Raquel Welch.

But nothing was more wonderful than the love and support of my family.

CHAPTER 34

THE THINKER

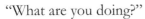

"What are you doing?"

Susie will ask me this from time to time as I sit quietly (or even stand as if I'm frozen to the spot). The dialogue then usually goes along the lines of.

"I'm thinking"

"You've spent ages 'thinking'"

"Yes, that's because I haven't finished yet"

This thoughtful and introspective nature stems from the fact that, as a young child, I spent quite a lot of time alone. My sister Joyce was born ten years after me so most of our childhoods were separate and quite a lot of mine was spent 'solo'.

I played outside, of course, as most kids did but in evening hours and dark winter days, I read books, many of which I'd find challenging today. My prizes at Berwick Grammar School (and I won quite a few) were book tokens. My collection of prize winning and 'serious' books still sit on our bookshelves; classics by Charles Dickens and adventure stories by Robert Louis Stevenson and Rider Haggard. All leather covered books with tight small print and narrow line spacing designed for the serious reader, obviously.

I also enjoyed more trivial books but didn't use my award-winning vouchers on these. I'm not sure if that was my decision alone or whether my Dad had an influence. Richmal Crompton's 'William' stories, Agatha Christie novels and textual comics like 'Wizard' and 'Hotspur' and their associated 'Annuals' sit on my shelves too.

My thinking nature meant that I spent hours listening to radio (I loved radio plays and serials) and I could even get enjoyment from my Dansette record player with only one or two records. These activities gave lots of scope for imagination and dreaming.

At my school/parent reviews, teachers would tell my Mam and Dad that I was an intelligent boy. I was never described as being 'knowledgeable'. Having been advised (i.e. forced) to cut my subjects to focus on a selected few didn't help - it limited my access to knowledge and had an impact on my development. Even today, I'm pretty hopeless at history, geography and many aspects of English literature, for example.

But I am intelligent (allegedly)

So how is this thing called intelligence measured? I'm pretty certain it isn't just about being a deep and frequent thinker.

In 1912, a German Psychologist (William Stern) came up with the idea of 'intelligence quotient' as a measure of intelligence. This IQ was a ratio of mental age versus chronological age multiplied by 100 to give a number. Mensa is the largest and oldest high IQ society in the world. It is a non-profit organization open to people who score at the 98th percentile or higher on a standardized, supervised IQ or other approved intelligence test. That's the marketing blurb anyway.

High intelligence cannot be a measure of common sense as I got lost trying to get to the test location on the day of my exam. However, I managed to persuade them to let me try again on another date – not only intelligent but persuasive too!

I took my Mensa test in my early fifties and I was awarded an IQ score of 145.

As my chronological age has increased by a couple of decades since I took the test, if my IQ is still the same, it must mean that my mental age has increased accordingly. I don't intend to retest myself; instead, I'll support the view that you get wiser as you get older.

Quite a few celebrity folks have high IQ scores and are Mensa members: Geena Davis, Quentin Tarrantino, Sharon Stone, Steve Martin and scores of lesser known individuals. I joined Mensa to prove to myself I could and maybe too, if I'm being honest, to be able to show off a little.

I'm a bit embarrassed to admit that, for a while, I carried my Mensa membership card sticking out of a pocket in my briefcase so it could be 'noticed'.

"Oh, yes, that's my Mensa membership card; I wondered where it was"

The novelty wore off after a short while; there were local and national meetings (how boring!) but it was an expensive way of getting four Mensa magazines a year. I dropped out when it became time to pay another year's membership fee.

During my time running Cambridge Associates training courses, I became qualified to teach the 'Myers Briggs Personality Indicator' (MBTI). One assessment measurement put me on the cusp between 'introversion; and 'extraversion'. In MBTI terms, this scale defines where you get your sources of energy and stimulation (it isn't about whether you are gregarious or quiet). Everything I've learned about myself convinces me that I am genuinely on the borderline here. On the one hand, I love performing and feeling the audience enjoyment. On the other hand. I like to think things through for myself and create my own ideas and action plans; I'm not the best team player in this regard.

For better or for worse I think I have passed my 'thinking' tendencies to Lucy. She has a full set of the 'Freeman' 'deep thinking' skills and she certainly didn't get them from her mother (better attributes kicked in from that source).

The more I write these memoir notes, the more I see myself as a true 'Janus man'. I am part outgoing person who revels being in the public eye and I am part solitude lover who get a lot of enjoyment from thinking and daydreaming.

What does all that mean for me?

I'll need to think about that a bit more.

CHAPTER 35

BIRCH HILL CARE HOME

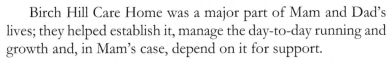

Birch Hill Care Home was a major part of Mam and Dad's lives; they helped establish it, manage the day-to-day running and growth and, in Mam's case, depend on it for support.

The house was set up in march 1970, in Norham village, as a holiday home for members of the motor trade but, over the years, has also become a residential care home with support for Alzheimer and dementia patients.

BEN, as the trade benevolent society is known, started in 1905 to help people who were having difficult times. The society owns and runs several homes and this one in Norham was opened in the late nineteen sixties.

When we moved to Norham in 1955, the house was owned by the Crawhall family; one of the well-to-do village families who operated at higher social circles than we did. I knew Mickey Crawhall, the son; he was a few years older than me and went to a prestigious boarding school but he would play with us local boys from time to time.

Dad had worked in the motor trade and was, therefore, a BEN member. As the only one in our area, he liaised with the association during the process of finding the house and then helping BEN set it up.

The timing worked well for our family as Mam spent time at Birch Hill recuperating from her heart surgery (December 1971) and, at the suggestion of her doctor, got involved in preparing menus and meals for residents. These activities suited her both medically and practically as she had been the local school cook some years before.

The original manageress had departed over a conflict of style (her prison management experience was deemed a bit too severe!) and as Mam got more involved, she eventually took over the role and became manageress in 1972 - with Dad as main backup and support.

Every time I visited Norham, Birch Hill became my second home; Driving from the south, my car took me there automatically where I was invariably fed with whatever fare was on the go. We slept at 11 St Cuthberts' Square but spent time at Birch Hill and had meals in the staff kitchen. Mam and Dad often stayed overnight at the house as live-in overnight staff. Lots of local people worked at the house and there was a good relationship with the community. Those were the fun days. The house is now much more of a dementia care home with full time professional staff.

Joyce, my sister, tells me that as Dad was lifetime member of BEN, I have an automatic right to a resident place if I need it. It's a bit remote from the rest of my family so I'm not intending to exercise that right. They might prefer that I went 'ga-ga' three hundred miles away from them, but I'm banking on the high fees being a disincentive to them sending me away.

My memories of Birch Hill are a bit hazy but I recall lots of food, laughter, accordion playing, bingo games (more on that in a moment) and lively Christmas parties. The residents were old, some were infirm but they knew how to enjoy a party.

I remember a few characters – Mabel, the dear old girl who smoked a pipe, Archie, a wandering accordion player, Little Ernie who walked the dog and a saucy old ex-dancer (sounds like my wife) who, due to dementia had lost her inhibitions and insisted on showing her knickers to every man who came nearby (sounds like my wife even more!).

Dad worked tirelessly (and free of charge) planning and managing the building of an extension with several self-contained rooms and apartments. He organised the suppliers and coordinated a lot of the work. I have memories and photographs of him digging soil, planting shrubs etc.

The extension was formally opened in 1975 by Princess Alexandra (the patron of BEN fund) and her husband Angus Ogilvy. I wasn't there but my sister, Joyce, assumed her rightful role in the pecking order working in the background to serve drinks and buffet lunches to the guests. There's a photo of my parents with these Royal Guests at the opening ceremony hanging in our hallway at home.

Photo records at Birch Hill show Angus Ogilvy sitting with Mabel, smoking their respective pipes and no doubt discussing the merits of various tobaccos.

A few years after Dad died, Mam eventually needed support and became a full-time resident in care. She had contributed so much to the house and fully deserved to reap the benefits of her work.

Over the years, dementia took its toll and Mam became increasingly confused but I'm thankful she always recognised Joyce and me and that my children got to know her – and still remember her with love; xxx Mam.

The more challenged residents, who needed extra care, had a separate sitting room and dining area. I can remember sitting around a table with Mam and other residents to play bingo. Each of the participants had a helper to play on their behalf. These games were fun and, more often than not, the residents would have nodded off to sleep leaving the carers to continue the game on their own.

Joyce and I (and, to a lesser extent, Susie, Tom and Lucy) have fond memories of Birch Hill and are grateful that it came along at a time that was right for our parents. It gave Dad a valuable purpose and role and was a lifeline for Mam's recovery post surgery.

Mam always spoke her mind and wasn't afraid to cross swords with the BEN establishment to do what she believed was right for Birch Hill. Despite these skirmishes, she was recognised as a special person who had given immense value to the home.

Some months after she passed away, Joyce and I were proud, in April 1997, to be part of the ceremony inaugurating the 'Margaret Freeman Room' in her honour and placing the named plaque on the door.

There's also a plaque near a newly planted tree in the driveway 'dedicated to Bob and Margaret Freeman'.

There is an ongoing challenge for care homes today. Dementia and Alzheimer diseases are truly awful and can be more of a stress to relatives than to the recipients. The hope that we all have (that I certainly have!) is to age with self-respect and, when the time comes, to die with grace, dignity and with minimum stress on my family members.

The award-winning book 'Being Mortal' tells us that our lives are like stories – we want to be author of our own tale and every one of these needs a satisfactory ending. We need places and support to help people with their 'life endings' and not just to medically keep them alive. Birch Hill, thanks to Bob and Margaret Freeman strives to do that.

A slightly serious tone there but it makes me realise that, in writing this story about my life, I am approaching the final chapter and that I haven't quite yet worked out the punchline.

CHAPTER 36

SIXTIES 'COOL'

◆•————————————•————————————•◆

"'Engerland' swings like a pendulum do ..." so went the popular Roger Miller 1965 song that epitomised the 'cool Britannia' image of the day. The ballad continued "Bobbies on bicycles two by two". A quaint image but one I've never seen - except in old black and white movies and the PC49 cartoon strips in the 'Eagle' comic.

I'm not convinced that Roger Miller had a close link with the real world given that one of his previous hits was called, 'You can't roller-skate through a buffalo herd'.

There was something exciting about 'the sixties', both at the time I lived through those years and in the media hyped up memories that I have. This was the decade that I started as a sixteen-year-old struggling to cope with awkward fumbled romantic attempts and ended as a twenty-six-year-old still struggling with awkward fumbled romantic attempts.

My second year at Bristol University, in 1963, was the time Beatlemania started; away went the Brylcreemed quiffs of piled up top hair (yes, I had some!) to be replaced by a Paul McCartney style fringe. A few of the trend following students adopted the Beatles style rounded collar jackets whereas I was just getting comfortable with the left-wing rebellious Donkey jacket image.

My final University year, in the mid-sixties, was anything but cool. At least in terms of accommodation. I, and three friends, inhabited a basement flat at 12A Royal York Crescent, Clifton; a fashionable Georgian Crescent but our flat was an accommodation disaster waiting to happen. It was a two bedroomed basement cellar with only a single entrance / exit. This basement cellar flat had a basement floor below it with only a single entrance / exit. Two levels of danger!

Our landlord was a nice old chap, probably in his seventies, who kept giving us his, rather insipid, watercolour paintings to hang on our walls. It seemed discourteous not to take them.

What sort of landlord likes to stuff his rental property with his own paintings? Oops, I seem to fit that category at our Heacham Beach house – but, at least, I'm trying to sell them.

Our Royal York Crescent basement flat had one of those (now deemed dangerous) gas hot water things. The kind that goes 'woomph' when you turn on the flame to heat the water. It worked OK but there was always a smell of gas. I think it was gas, maybe it was carbon monoxide.

Susie went to drama school in Bristol (we didn't overlap) and on one of our visits a few years ago, I took her to see where I lived. I was obviously trying to impress her and prove that I had been a sixties cool dude. The place had been transformed; it looked very smart on the outside and presumably the inside was just as impressive. It would then be compliant with all residential safety standards and no longer a home for our ex-landlord's paintings.

The swinging sixties were in their heyday when I moved to London to start my first 'proper job' at IBM. After a brief hiccup to sort out somewhere to live, I landed at the most prestigious address that I am likely to have. This was the top floor flat at 50 Montague Square – postcode 'W1'. None of these extra letters and numbers featured in modern postcodes. Just 'W1' plain and simple – and prestigious.Ringo Starr, wife Maureen and baby Zak lived a few houses from us. He owned the whole house and wasn't renting a top floor flat but, hey, we were neighbours.

Telephone numbers were distinctive too before the growth in demand categorised them in a boring way. We were 'Ambassador 4254'. On the handset you dialled 'AMB4254'; the rotary dial had letters as well as numbers. This was pre the '01-4254' classification (which was followed by '071-4254' and a few years later by '0207-4254'. I haven't tried to dial these versions; they might not exist. Besides, my flatmates don't live there anymore.

The ground floor housed a posh man who, in my two years, I never saw not wearing a formal suit (I didn't see him much though). The middle floor housed Major Rymer and his wife. He was in his fifties at a guess; very military in his bearing and drove a topless MGB sports car. A sort of John Steed character played by Patrick Macnee in 'The Avengers' TV. We had little contact with him either apart from the time when my flatmate, Bob Marshall-Andrews knocked a milk bottle from our window ledge on to his balcony. I wasn't involved in this but, judging by the expression on the major's face when he peered up at me while Bob swept up the debris, I suspect I was being put in the guilty frame.

I had a surprise encounter with Alan Price on a sunbed in a High Street Kensington tanning shop. This would be nineteen seventy or thereabouts. We are wary of ultra-violet rays today but in those days, it was quite common, fashionable even, to build up a sun tan. The tanning sessions worked well for me preparing my skin for holidays in the sun and for sunbathing at home. I liked going to the tanning centre as glamorous people dropped by seeking beauty treatment. I also liked it because I had a brief fling with the receptionist Vicky Schofield. If you are out there Vicky, I'm sorry I stopped coming.

At one session, I was put into a booth with two suntan beds and Alan Price was already there. He was preparing for a film (or 'filum', as his Geordie accent would have it) and needed to look healthy. He was the lead man in 'Alfie Darling', a follow up to the 1966 'Alfie' movie starring Michael Caine. It was a darker story and a very much inferior movie. I'm glad you took my advice and kept your music career going, Alan!

Carnaby Street became the trendy area for clothing and other weird stuff that claimed to be fashionable. Not my scene at all bult it was colourful and lively with lots of coffee bars. One glamorous mini-skirted shop assistant persuaded me to have a shirt custom made. It was in Neil Diamond style with high collar and billowing sleeves and looked great on him on a promotional poster (which inspired the idea). It looked ridiculous on me and was made from an uncomfortable silky material. I never wore it and years later it ended up in a charity shop.

The sixties years was the decade of Saturday night parties. I would play rugby in the afternoon, have a few beers and then, if I didn't have a date which was more often true than not, try to find a party to go to. Or just continue drinking beer before devouring a curry.

Looking for a party (if I hadn't been invited to one) meant trawling the streets of Kensington carrying a 'party four' (four pint) can of beer and looking for the sight and sound of a party we could gatecrash. In truth, it wasn't as random or wayward as it appears. Party-givers expected strangers to turn up uttering phrases like "Nigel said I should come" and we would smuggle our 'party four' beer can back to others as we went in giving the illusion of providing lots of beer.

Many parties were just vehicles to stand in someone's kitchen and drink beer beyond pub closing time.

Some parties were better than others; I recall meeting, and talking to, Chrissie Shrimpton (Jean Shrimpton's sister) and the Dave Clarke Five (or four really as DC wasn't there). None of them became lifelong friends but were good company for a while.

I was never a cool dude in a fashionable 'Cool Britannia' sense (or in any other sense, come to think of it) but I had the opportunity to come close. A colleague of mine owned an E-type jaguar and he was giving me a lift. We decided to cruise down Kings Road to see what we could see, maybe stop for a drink and try to 'chat up' girls. The car attracted attention and being very low slung was quite difficult to get out – especially if you are as tall as I am.

Outside a crowded bar seemed a good place to stop and project our cool-girl-pulling images to the people standing there. I opened the door and, instead of smiling at girls in anticipation of flirty chat, I should have been more careful where I placed my left hand on the pavement to help me get out instead of letting it slide in some dog shit.

Not the 'coolest' start to chatting and flirting.

CHAPTER 37

MY ECCENTRIC HOBBIES

◆•————————————•————————————•◆

On her wedding day my daughter Lucy described her parents as being eccentric. I'm sure she meant it fondly and there are some flattering definitions of this word; 'unconventional', 'special', 'unique'. Google also comes up with a few less complementary descriptions 'geeky', 'a crank', 'oddball' and 'viewed as having a screw loose'. I'll let others be the judge of what applies to me and confirm that my curiosity draws me into some unusual areas of interest.

I confess to being an 'impossible bottler' – i.e. one of the eccentric bunch of people that enjoys filling a bottle with items too large to pass through its neck. The 'ship-in-bottle' craze dates back to the early years of the nineteenth century and is now more a craft project than a mysterious black art.

My 1958 Scout Annual spilt the beans for me; you slide the folding model ship inside the bottle and pull a thread to raise the masts. You then burn this thread (to destroy the evidence) whilst making sure that nothing else catches fire – inside or outside of the bottle.

That latter step was the trickiest part.

For those readers still with me, Harry Eng (1932 – 96) started the cards-inside-a-bottle trend. He was a teacher, inventor, magician and puzzle fanatic. Rumour has it that after a lively dinner in a London hotel, he took an empty wine bottle to his room and produced it the following morning containing a pack of unopened playing cards, the hotel menu and a book of matches. History doesn't tell us if Harry's dining companions set this challenge but, in his lifetime, he produced over six hundred bottles containing a variety of items each wider than the container neck.

These 'impossible bottles', in Harry's eyes, were pieces of art intended to inspire people and to make them believe that anything is possible.

Even today, people suspect some kind of magical cheating. They shake the bottle, poke things inside it, look for a seam where the glass might have been cut and fused. When I point out that glass melts at over one thousand degrees Fahrenheit and that such a temperature would destroy the contents, they still challenge the method.

'Is this a clever magic trick?'

Nothing could be further from the truth. A good bottler will make sure that the pack of cards doesn't reveal signs of disassembly outside the bottle and subsequent reassembly inside.

There - I've blurted the secret. There are skills and careful handling involved, but there is no cheating and no magic. All serious bottlers stick to the 'rules' that Harry Eng established; the glass must not be cut or modified and everything inside the bottle must pass through its neck.

My contribution to the 'Impossible Bottle' saga is to personalise the item with a photograph on the front of the card box and an appropriate message written on the reverse. My bottles are popular with wedding couples and as a unique gift at the birth of a child.

A nice touch, even though I say so myself. I like to think Harry would have been pleased.

That hobby alone possibly wouldn't classify me as eccentric but when you add my 3D and 360-degree photography, I don't seem to be the typical, 'I'm going to the shed to saw some wood' kind of dad.

One of my early childhood presents was Viewmaster. I would be about eight years old when I got my first viewer and a circular reel of Caribbean island photos. Staring through the eyepieces and looking at a three-dimensional picture swept me into flights of imagination. That single reel kept me happy for a long time. I've now got dozens of reels and via my 3D camera make new ones. I don't physically make them myself; I send the images to an equally nerdy colleague who does.

Brian May, the queen guitarist, is an authority on stereographic photography and has one of the biggest collections of stereographic cards. These look like postcards with two photograph images, one for the left eye and one for the right, and you need an appropriate viewer to see the image in its three-dimensional glory. 3D photography has been around since Victorian times and predates the single image version we have today. My collection of stereocards is paltry compared to that of Brian May.

He's obviously a bigger geek than me – and, rumour has it, a better musician too.

I could talk about my obsession with Eagle comics, Dan Dare and Jeff Hawke cartoons and wind-up train sets, to say nothing about my occasional balloon-modelling and attempts at magic but that might make me seem genuinely eccentric.

And I'm not.

In any case, these things will sort themselves out when I finally grow up.

I promise.

CHAPTER 38

JOB DONE, NOW WHAT?

◆━━━━━━━━━━━━━━●━━━━━━━━━━━●◆

There's a well know quotation attributed to John Lennon:

"When I was 5 years old, my mother always told me that happiness was the key to life. When I went to school, they asked me what I wanted to be when I grew up. I wrote down 'happy'. They told me I didn't understand the assignment, and I told them they didn't understand life."

There's some doubt as to whether John originated these words or just remembered and repeated them.

Either way, the quotation strikes a chord with me and, as I reflect on my life, the things I find meaningful are nothing to do with wealth or status (thankfully!) but in the joy of having helped establish a wonderful family (thankfully again).

Like most people, I never had a clear set of ambitions or life goals (does anyone?); I tended to just go with the flow, to try to enjoy it and to make the best of it.

Our children, Tom and Lucy are now adult and established so, to quote my dad, 'Job Done'. The job is never 'done' of course and neither Susy or I would want it to be. Every parent enjoys being asked for an opinion or for some advice even though we know that our 'children' are now highly capable and grown up adults. I can speak for Susy and say that we are so proud of them both and the lives they have made for themselves.

Do I have any regrets? Would I change anything if I could? I certainly wouldn't change the results of my life and my only regrets concern my behaviour during parts of it. I've shouted at my children; I've broken toys and I've made them cry and these memories still haunt me. Late one night I gave Lucy calamine lotion instead of medicine and only saw my error when she complained it 'tasted yukky'. I immediately took some myself so as to share any consequence that I had put on her. It did, indeed, taste 'yukky' but there were no after effects.

Continuing the theme of 'regrets'; it brings tears to my eyes to think about how I selfishly ignored my parents. It was a lousy reward for Mam who had always been a 'rock in a pinny' and Dad who was my guide to 'right and wrong'. I really wish I could say 'sorry' for my selfish behaviour but who doesn't wish they could 'say something' to their departed parents? I don't think I would win the 'best brother' award either as I have been unnecessarily rude and curt with Joyce many times but I know she's forgiven me!

I think my errant behaviour was, in part, caused by a 'bad' marriage; I haven't dwelt on that topic which is best confined to history; the only good thing about it is that it occupied my time until I met Susie; the love of my life and my 'rock without a pinny'.

The 'Sliding Doors' on that occasion did me a favour! If I had my time again, I wouldn't change anything apart from aspects of my behaviour. I would want to make sure that I got the same outcome.

My family is my proud legacy.

Printed in Great Britain
by Amazon

57565935R00092